Devon is a transformation powerhouse who has a contagious energy and passionate zest for life. As an author, speaker, and coach he has committed his purpose to helping people to get unstuck, inspiring them to transform their life with a focus on achieving breakthrough in the areas of mindset and relationships. A successful serial entrepreneur across media and luxury property sectors, Devon knows what it's like to feel stuck. He turned his life around, from battling the crippling effects of alcoholism and addiction, hating the man he saw in the mirror, to living a life of purpose, love, and serving others through his experience.

This book is dedicated to three phenomenal women who stood by my side throughout my journey of healing and transformation: Chelsea Lynne Grey, Jade Porter and Ingi Brough.

Devon Brough

GET OVA IT!

A REAL LIFE SOLUTION TO GET
UNSTUCK AND BREAK FREE

AUSTIN MACAULEY PUBLISHERS™

LONDON * CAMBRIDGE * NEW YORK * SHARJAH

A CIP catalogue record for this title is available from the British Library.

ISBN 9781398429338 (Paperback)
ISBN 9781398429345 (ePub e-book)

www.austinmacauley.com

First Published 2023
Austin Macauley Publishers Ltd®
1 Canada Square
Canary Wharf
London
E14 5AA

I am nothing without the loving presence of God in my life. All credit goes to Him for blessing me with a purpose to serve.

A huge shoutout to my community on Instagram. Your constant engagement and encouragement is why I do what I do.

A massive thanks to my publisher, Tim Richman, and his team at Burnet Media, who have guided me through the entire process. In particular, thanks to Nicola, the most phenomenal editor, who brought my words to life on the page.

I am who I am today because of the love and support I constantly receive from my closest friends: Chelsea Lynne Grey, Jade Porter, Gina Brown, Nikita Wright, Nicola Loots, Nicole Halvey and Lindy Kühn.

Table of Contents

Introduction
Breaking Free and Breaking Through

Growth is painful. Change is painful. But nothing is as painful as staying stuck where you don't belong.
– NR Narayan Murthy

I spent most of my early adult life in fear. There was no light at the end of my proverbial tunnel—if there had been, it would have been from a freight train heading straight towards me.

Hopeless is the only word I can use to describe how I felt during those years.

When I was born, my grandfather, who delivered me, had to break my mother's pelvis so I could fit through. But the pain I caused my mother that day was tiny in comparison to the pain I would cause her and those closest to me—and myself—for many years to come.

My birth aside, the mess that used to be my life really began when I was 15. At that young age, I was dared by my friends to down a bottle of tequila. I made it halfway before I physically couldn't drink any more. I went home that night in a drunken stupor, falling and vomiting pretty much everywhere. My mother was angry, understandably so, and I remember standing in the corner of my room as she shouted at me, coming closer. I hit out in front of me and ended up punching my own mother in the face, shattering her cheek bone.

I had just experienced for the first time how aggressive I became under the influence of alcohol.

A few years later, at the age of 19, I was duped into a cheque-book scam by my best friend at the time, someone who was like a brother to me. A cheque for a substantial amount of money was deposited into my account and I was driven around to buy items like car rims, tyres and expensive alcohol, which I paid for with my own personal cheques. A week later I was at a supermarket writing out a cheque for a large purchase of groceries when I was abruptly taken to the manager's office and kept there until three policemen arrived. They arrested me, and I discovered I had a total of 18 warrants out for my arrest for financial fraud. The cheque that had been deposited into my account had bounced—and, with it, all of my cheques.

My supposed best friend got me out of the holding cell that night illegally—he knew some powerful people—but what ensued was a nightmare. I couldn't go home to my mother's house, as the cops would track me down there. The only person who offered to help was a Russian man who ran a brothel. For an entire year, I hid in one of his homes, along with three of his prostitutes. I had no freedom and lived in absolute terror of going to jail. To avoid possible roadblocks and the potential of 12 years' imprisonment on white-collar charges, I was unable to drive myself anywhere. I was understandably stressed out and desperate, and my drinking and drug use spiralled out of control. Over the course of a year, I managed to pay back all the money by working as a freelance editor in the television industry—but alcohol and drugs had become my crutch.

Of course, there were consequences—for those around me and for myself. In my twenties, alcoholism and addiction held me in a crippling cycle of anger, resentment, guilt and shame. I believed deeply that I was undeserving and unworthy of success or love, and so I found myself sabotaging and destroying everything good in my life. I hurt the people closest to me and left a path of destruction wherever I went.

I mastered the art of self-hatred—I couldn't stand the man looking back at me in the mirror. Through my own thoughts and self-talk, I convinced myself that I was my own worst enemy, and so I constantly beat myself up, using every opportunity to remind myself that I was an alcoholic, an addict, a failure, a fuck-up, a useless waste of human life.

I could never be in silence. Whether I was at home or driving in my car, the radio or TV had to be blaring to drown out my abusive inner dialogue. Quietness allowed that ever-present demon on my shoulder to regurgitate stories about my incompetence and many shortcomings.

I was aware of what was going on—that drinking and drugs were destroying my life—and I hated feeling so stuck. As I descended deeper to desperate levels of despair and hopelessness, I tried to commit suicide—not once, but twice. The first time I was 22, the second I was 26. Both times I honestly felt there was no hope left, that there would never be any relief from my inner turmoil. Just being awake was painful. The idea of not having to face my own self felt like it would liberate me. Isolated, lonely, scared and desperate for a reprieve, I was convinced that breathing one more breath, living one more day, would be more torturous than ending it all.

> "Your desire to change must be greater than your desire to stay the same."
>
> – Unknown

I was truly suffering—but I was such a failure that I couldn't even get suicide right. So trust me that I know from experience there is no greater pain than the pain of feeling stuck.

The good news is that every one of us has the capacity to create change—even me! With the right tools and enough desire, we all have the ability to break through the shackles that keep us stuck. Right now, you too have everything it takes to break free from the things that are holding you back, and move towards a life of joy, fulfilment, growth, purpose, success and love.

In my early thirties, I finally reached my rock bottom. After a six-day bender of booze, cocaine and crystal meth, life brought me to my knees. I had no options left and I was exhausted. Driven by total despair, I finally

> "Rock bottom has built more champions than privilege ever did."
>
> – Unknown

surrendered and cried out for help. With the support of my mother, brother and aunt, I booked myself into an in-patient rehabilitation centre.

I will never forget the day I arrived. It was 7 October 2016, the day my life started to turn around.

The four months I spent in rehab—over Christmas and New Year 2016, living with more than 50 other alcoholics and addicts—were life-changing. I actually wanted to be there. I was desperate for a new life and prepared to do whatever it took to break the cycle. I faced my demons, confronted the pain I'd been running from for so long. In that space, I was forced to unpack and dissect the events, thoughts, feelings, behaviours and narratives that had kept me stuck.

I left the treatment centre on 26 January 2017 equipped with tools to face life on life's terms, with a renewed mindset, and a passionate fire burning in my belly to step into my purpose and create the life of my dreams.

I immediately went to work, rebuilding my life. In 2018, I entered the real-estate market, and started sourcing and structuring land deals for some of the largest luxury property developers in South Africa. A year later, still clean and sober, I launched a division of a real-estate agency with a partner. In 2020, amid Covid-19 and international lockdowns, we found ourselves in the toughest property market since the 2008 global financial crisis. Nevertheless, we achieved a staggering sales turnover of a little under R700-million ($46-million) after just 24 months of operation.

In four years, I had turned my life around by following a precise, well-crafted formula. I had completely transformed myself. Today, I'm a luxury property developer and consultant, having presented over R1-billion in deal value since coming out of rehab.

Other areas of my life have also flourished. The last five years of sobriety have been a beautiful adventure as I have discovered who I am and who I want to be, and undertaken a personal search for meaning and purpose. By openly sharing my story, I started to form deep connections and friendships with incredible people. I now have a rock-solid VIP support structure and the most amazing group of close-knit friends.

My life now is unrecognisable from the chaos of my twenties and early thirties. Today, it is filled with love—love for others, love for everything I do, and love for myself. I've moved into a space of flow, where anxiety and stress are greatly reduced, and where the constant battle against the tide of life is a mere memory.

I wrote this book to share my experience and the simple process I repeated to get from where I was before to where I am today. And I feel it is my God-given purpose to help you break free from anything that is holding you back from experiencing the best that life has to offer.

Get OVA It is the process of stacking Ownership, Vision and Action to get "OVA" the pain, challenges and obstacles that keep you stuck. It is such a simple blueprint that absolutely anyone can use it, no matter your level of growth or awakening. I have found that it can be applied in any area of life and used in almost any situation.

I'm going to show you how I finally took ownership of my past and the mess I had created, how I crafted a vision for where I wanted to be, and how I took action in order to build momentum and experience consistent results.

This methodology will help you achieve your breakthrough so you too can experience the joy and satisfaction of seeing progress and results. The by-product is a heightening of self-worth as you add value not only to your own life, but to the lives of those around you.

As you let go of all the baggage that has weighed so heavily on your shoulders, you will begin to fall in love with yourself. You will wake up in the morning excited to pursue your purpose, and you will be equipped to consistently take disciplined action towards achieving your goals and dreams.

"I don't care what you've done or who you've been. All that matters is who you want to be, and what you're willing to sacrifice in order to become that person."
– Tom Bilyeu

You will contribute to the world around you—and I guarantee that in a few years you will look back and not recognise the life you used to live.

The process of change begins with one simple decision. It truly doesn't matter what you've done or who you've been—there is tremendous power when you decide that you've had enough of being stuck. And hey, maybe right now is that moment for you!

I'd love you to stay in touch along this journey. Find me on Instagram @devonbroughsa, and feel free to browse through the videos I post to help you along the way. You can tag me or drop me a DM to share parts of your story as you progress through this book.

Welcome to an epic quest of inner mastery, an adventure that will continue to unfold for the rest of your life!

The Basics
The Three Pillars of the OVA Method

Ownership, vision and action—three incredibly powerful words. You will have definitely heard of them, individually, as effective tools for growth. The secret is how you use them, and in particular how you combine them: they become exponentially more powerful when stacked together and used in this particular order.

In the three parts of this book, I explore each of these concepts and how they can dramatically affect you, liberating you from suffering and propelling you towards your dream life. Let's explore these ideas here before we begin.

Ownership

In its purest form, ownership is about taking responsibility for your past experiences and present state. It begins with awareness. First, awareness of your emotional attachment to past events and the narrative you've created in relation to them. And second, awareness of your thoughts, feelings and actions as events unfold in the present moment.

When you take full ownership of your life, you accept that you are 100% accountable for your inner state of being at any time.

You understand that, regardless of circumstance, you have the power to determine your own narrative. If you choose to, you can shift the meaning you've attached to past life events, and instead of being a victim, you can become a victor.

When you adopt a mindset of radical ownership, you no longer blame or complain. You start to see that the role you have played in every situation has brought you to where you are right now.

In Part 1, I'll show you how every single experience you've had in the past was perfect for you today; that everything that happens to you is exactly what you need in order to wake up and grow. It is an absolute truth that you grow through pain, obstacles and challenges. To uncover the hidden lessons and blessings in every event, circumstance and experience, you need to face them head-on. If you run away from these uncomfortable situations, you deny your self-growth.

There is purpose in pain. Pain is a feeling we often try to avoid, but the primary purpose of pain is to push us to take action. By avoiding pain, you rob yourself of your chance to grow. I am going to teach you how to embrace your pain, and how to flip the script and use pain to serve yourself and others.

You cannot "un-experience" a traumatic or painful event that has happened in the past, but when you take ownership, you realise that you have the power to shift your perspective and embrace a healthier relationship and emotional attachment to that event. Instead of seeing it as a setback, you can change the meaning you attach to it and see how it has set you up for your greater purpose.

I will show you how to address the four heaviest emotions that have the potential to keep you stuck—anger, resentment, guilt and shame—because if they are not converted to healthier emotions, they can restrain you in a toxic cycle of victimhood.

You are the author of your own story, and the beauty of this is that you have full control in rewriting your narrative—not just for future chapters, but also for any past experiences that don't sit right with you at the moment. When you learn how to shift your perspective, you can transform the narrative of any event or situation from a disempowering one that keeps you stuck and bitter to an empowering one that helps you grow and makes you better.

Growth isn't just about learning more or picking up new tools—it's also about learning how to let go of what no longer serves you. This is why it's so important to start this work with the concept of ownership: it won't help to craft a vision for your future, or take action, if you're still holding on to baggage that weighs you down. Skipping this vital step is like climbing Mount Everest wearing a 100-kilogram backpack. You won't even make it to base camp.

Starting with the core pillar of ownership helps us cast off the heavy backpacks we so often carry so we can appreciate the view: a bright and beautiful future. And this leads us to the second pillar…

Vision

A GPS cannot take you anywhere unless you first put in your destination. Or, to put it another way, without a clear vision, you're like a boat with no rudder and no sails, bobbing around the ocean of life, being washed wherever the waves take you.

Without a vision you will feel like you're on autopilot, in a holding pattern or just going round in circles—which is frustrating, right? Because without progress, you feel stuck. (It's the same as when you're caller #24 on the phone to your insurance company... Shoot me now.)

That's why you have to get absolute clarity on what you want in all areas of your life. In the absence of a clear and strong vision for your future, you easily become addicted to memories from your past. One pitfall is that we often know with absolute clarity what we don't want—and this, ironically, can be why we attract even more of exactly that into our lives.

Using the power of vision, you can tap into the powerful energy that comes from being a co-creator of your life and an architect of your future—which sounds far better than being a bystander and just seeing what happens.

In Part 2, I'm going to show you how to craft a vision that is authentic to you—one that will get you out of bed in the morning, excited to create, and see momentum build in every area of your life. We'll explore your life's vision, mission and purpose, and interrogate how this will serve your ultimate purpose: serving others.

I'll share tools to keep your vision top of mind and constantly evolving as you grow into the new person that you are destined to become.

Vision isn't just about the things you want to have, it's also about who you want to be. Once you know where you're headed, you can be held accountable for the third step...

Action

Once you've taken radical ownership of your life and have crafted a compelling vision that excites you to the core, the next and final step is the hardest—and it's where most people fall short. It's where you get to work and take action.

Action is the most potent ingredient of the "OVA" formula, because it activates the work and brings it to life. This is where the pedal hits the metal.

In Part 3, we look at fear, procrastination, distraction, people and perfectionism. I'll dissect some of the most potent roadblocks we all encounter when it comes to taking action in our lives, and the reasons why we get stuck there.

To get OVA the barriers that lie in the way of taking action, you're going to need discipline—and discipline is built one task at a time. I'll show you how you can take your life's vision and break it down into achievable, manageable and sustainable steps.

These days, we all seek instant gratification. Social media shows us someone else's success, and we expect to see the same results instantly in our own lives. We get discouraged when, after a few days of effort, our new business hasn't earned us a million-dollar contract.

But that just isn't how life works.

The key is to start small. When people say, "Rome wasn't built in a day," the next logical step is to realise that they were laying bricks every hour.

Often, we wake up and think, "Right, I'm going to change my life today. I'm going to cut out alcohol, start at the gym, eat healthily, take on a new hobby and work on my relationship with my mother." By setting so many ambitious goals all at once, we instantly make our end goal unattainable. Then, when we fall off the wagon, we reaffirm the narrative that we're incapable of change. We'll go on to explore comfort versus calling and pain versus pleasure, and then how your brain really works and why it often works against you, convincing you to do things that are bad for you and talking you out of doing the things that are best for you.

Growth comes from being persistent and not giving up, especially in the beginning. Little by little, a little adds up to a lot. And after a bit of time, if you stick to your plan, stay focused on your vision and take accountability for showing up with excellence, you will look back and marvel at what has been achieved.

Action creates momentum. I'm going to discuss the habits, rituals and routines of peak performers that create a state and attitude of excellence in body, mind and soul.

Are you excited? Ready for a massive change in your life?

Great, let's get started and jump right in to help you turn OVA a new leaf!

TAKE ACTION!

There is tremendous power in writing ideas on paper—it creates awareness and helps you identify the patterns that are emerging. So keep a journal and pen with you. Throughout this book, every time you see Take action!, stop reading, and take some time to think about the questions and write out your thoughts.

To download a PDF template for all the exercises, visit: *devonbrough.com/get-ova-it.*

Part 1
Ownership

When a team takes ownership of its problems, the problem gets solved. It is true on the battlefield, it is true in business, and it is true in life.
– Jocko Willink

In the corporate world, when you are asked to take ownership of a project, you're being asked to be accountable—you are the person responsible for the project's success. In your life, you have to be accountable for the most important project you could ever work on: Project YOU! And you are the only person responsible for its success.

In this section, we explore how we perceive and relate to the outside world, the meaning we attach to events, and how our inner state has a powerful effect on our outer world.

By the end of this section, you will understand the true purpose of pain, how your brain keeps you stuck, and why you hold on to feelings from the past that don't serve you. I'll show you how to rewrite the stories you keep telling yourself so you can foster an empowered mindset that will set you up for success on the rest of your journey.

Chapter 1
Awareness

The first step towards change is awareness.
The second step is acceptance.
– Nathaniel Branden

Without awareness there can be no growth, because you cannot fix something you don't know is broken. To become aware is to open your eyes, open your mind and open your heart—to observe what's going on outside you and to feel what is within you. Having awareness means having the ability to witness your thoughts and feelings as objectively as possible—to acknowledge what is really going on.

In the words of American pastor Robert Madu, "You cannot change what you cannot see." He describes a person having a kale salad for lunch, and then going about their day, busy with meetings and chores. That evening they get home and when they look in the mirror, they're dismayed to see a big green piece of kale stuck in their teeth. They think back to all the meetings they've had and the people they've spoken to, and they wonder why nobody said anything. They could've picked it out in a single second, but they didn't know it was there.

> What is necessary to change a person is to change his awareness of himself."
> – Abraham Maslow

They didn't take action, because they couldn't see the problem.

Pastor Madu also makes the comparison between a microscope and a mirror. It's easy to spot flaws in other people, to look at their life in minute detail through the lens of a microscope, dissecting every little thing they say and do. But when it comes to self-awareness, we need to swap the microscope for a mirror.

Looking in the mirror is scary. Becoming conscious of ourselves is difficult, and many people shy away from doing it because they're afraid of what they might find. They know that dealing with their stuff requires a lot of hard work. Once you see your destructive patterns in detail and understand how they influence your life and the lives of those close to you, you aren't able to stand idly by—you're compelled to take action and to do something about it.

Because once you've seen something, it cannot be unseen.

With your eyes closed, you can draw comfort from being a victim. You can deflect, blame and complain. But the path of least resistance is also the path towards personal destruction. Passing the buck is far easier than taking responsibility and actually fixing what isn't right.

I know from personal experience just how easy it is to avoid self-examination. For years, when a negative thought or feeling surfaced, I would drink and use drugs rather than look deeper.

> "With awareness comes responsibility and choice."
> – Amanda Lindhout

Not looking at my stuff meant I avoided taking responsibility and accountability—an unconscious, self-destructive path that led only to self-judgment and self-hatred.

Awakening is the process we go through when we become aware. At some point, I had to open my eyes to regain consciousness: without an awakening, I would probably still be stuck on my path of self-destruction.

Becoming conscious is the process of gaining awareness, not only of events that have taken place, but also of the meaning we have attached to those events. Later I'll show you how all events are neutral, but through our perception we attach meaning to them, and trigger subsequent thoughts and feelings that can keep us stuck, pull us backwards or propel us forward.

TAKE ACTION!
- What thoughts and feelings are you aware of right now?
- What life events from your past do you constantly think about?
- What drew you to this book, and where do you feel you are stuck?

Chapter 2
Our Evolutionary Disadvantage

Before we dig any deeper, we need to gain some understanding of the brain, the organ responsible for how we perceive and experience the world. When it comes to personal growth, we're already at a huge evolutionary disadvantage. The reptilian part of the brain is its oldest part, and it's also the first part to be activated when any external stimulus is triggered. It has one primary purpose: to keep us safe.

Since the beginning of time, it's the reptilian brain that has kept man alive in the face of a threat. When a wild animal appeared out of nowhere, the only question our reptilian brain would ask is, Am I in danger?

In its quest to seek safety, your brain is wired to trigger one of three responses: fight, flight or freeze. This millions-year-old habit is still active today, and it has a huge impact on our everyday lives. In the face of any perceived danger—even something like facing our own emotions, needing to have a hard conversation or dealing with a painful situation—we instinctively choose one of three options. We exert a massive amount of energy trying to gain control over the situation (fight), we turn and run (flight), or we are gripped with panic, fear and anxiety, unable to move or problem-solve (freeze). I'm sure you can relate to one or two or all three of these automatic responses.

In my own life, I created massive amounts of prolonged suffering by constantly fighting for control over, or running away from, the stuff I really needed to deal with. Alcohol was my escape—instead of facing my thoughts and feelings, I would drink. Instead of dealing with a personal conflict in a healthy way, I would drink. If a situation didn't go as planned, I would fight to try to control the outcome and then, frustrated when I didn't get my way, I would drink.

Fighting and running left me exhausted and frustrated—and continually fighting and running.

Then I discovered another way—and it's now my favourite F-word. Can you guess what it is? (Mind out of the gutter!)

The word is flow.

It takes time to get to a place of flow. We have to reprogramme our thinking, working against the instinctual patterns of our brain. This is not easy but, oh my, it is so rewarding when you finally enter your state of flow.

As you stop fighting life and begin to flow, you surrender and accept. You no longer run on instinct, reacting too quickly (often with catastrophic consequences). In flow, you discover the power that comes from embracing peace and calm. In this state, instead of just reacting to life, you respond in a collected, empowered way that serves your growth and what you want in your life.

TAKE ACTION!
- What situations or areas of your life are you desperately trying to control?
- What situations or events make you want to run away?
- What situations make you feel panic, fear and/or anxiety?
- How does this make you feel stuck?

Chapter 3
Being a Prisoner of Your Own Mind

Your mind can be either your prison or your palace.
What you make it is yours to decide.
– Bernard Kelvin Clive

The only place you get stuck is in your own head. Your own thinking can be your best friend or your worst enemy—which is why the most important discipline of ownership is mastering your mindset.

Our thoughts come and go throughout the day, often popping into our consciousness spontaneously, seemingly beyond our control. In 2005, the US National Science Foundation published a finding that people have an average of between 12 000 and 60 000 thoughts per day. Of these, 80% are negative and 95% are thoughts repeated from the day before.[1] So we tend to lean towards and repeat thoughts that cause stress, tension and exhaustion.

In The Laws of Human Nature, bestselling author Robert Greene explains in the very first chapter that humans are irrational by nature:

The first step towards becoming rational is to understand our fundamental irrationality. There are two factors that should render this more palatable to our egos: nobody is exempt from the irresistible effect of emotions on the mind, not even the wisest among us; and to some extent, irrationality is a function of the structure of our brains, and is wired into our very nature by the way we process emotions. Being irrational is almost beyond our control.

This is because our emotions and rational thinking are controlled by separate parts of our brain. When any event occurs, it's the emotional part of our brain that is triggered first. This is why we often react with emotional charge, before the rational part of the brain receives the signal and processes the event in a more logical manner.

Let's say you get home from work after a long day and your partner snaps at you in a way you don't like. Your kneejerk reaction may be to snap back—that's the emotional part of your brain, and it's pretty instantaneous. That leaves the rational part of your brain with no time to process the signal. If it did, it might pause to ask questions like, Why did my partner snap at me? Did something happen today? With this in mind, you may choose to be loving and compassionate, and to find out what's going on before reacting emotionally.

Snapping back at your partner may set off an argument that didn't need to happen. But if you give yourself a moment and allow your rational processing to kick in instead of automatically reacting, you'll have a greater chance of handling the situation from a place of calm and avoiding an unnecessary showdown.

TAKE ACTION!
- Are there certain people or situations that get under your skin and trigger an immediate reaction?
- Think of situations in which you automatically respond without thinking. How do you feel when this happens?
- How does your reaction serve the situation?
- Can you prepare yourself to look out for the warning signs of such situations, and so pre-empt them from happening in the first place?

Our brains are also habitual by nature. Author Dr Joe Dispenza, who has devoted a lot of time to the topic, puts it like this:

Ninety-five percent of who you are by the time you are 35 is a set of memorised behaviours and emotional reactions that create your identity subconsciously. Five percent of your conscious mind that is plugged into reality is working against 95% of what you've memorised subconsciously.[2]

When you allow this subconscious, automatic programme to dictate your thoughts and feelings, you become a prisoner of your own mind. When you allow those thoughts and feelings to dictate your actions, you are living on autopilot— you are reacting to life in ways that don't serve you.

Think of what it means to be a prisoner. You're confined to a limited space and controlled by external forces. It's the same if you don't take ownership of your thoughts, which are the language of your mind. Your own thinking keeps you confined and controls how you feel, which ultimately determines the actions you take in your life.

It's in the confines of your own mind—in your thinking—that you create your suffering. If you don't learn how to control your thoughts, they are left to their own devices. Even the smallest event can trigger thoughts that project a worst-case scenario, fuelling fear, anxiety and stress. If we allow our thoughts to run wild, we remain captive to a projection that isn't real and that often never even materialises.

Have you ever been around a person who is super-negative? They always expect the worst-case scenario and never see the good in anything. What does it feel like to be in their presence? It's heavy. You don't want to spend too much time with them.

Then take a person who is happy, joyful and optimistic. Even in a difficult situation they look for the silver lining; how they can learn and grow through the event. It feels good to spend time with them—their energy is contagious and it rubs off on you.

Which of these two people do you want to be?

Here's the good news: the prison door of your mind is standing wide open and you're the only warden on watch. If you learn to harness your thoughts by replacing the narrative you constantly tell yourself, you can shift from fear to faith, from anxiety to excitement, and from victim to victor.

When you take ownership of your own thinking and master your mindset, you can ease into a state of flow, where nothing outside of you can affect your inner state and being.

The key is to become aware of what thoughts you are feeding.

THE WOLF YOU FEED

One evening, an old Cherokee told his grandson about a fight that goes on inside people.

He said, "My son, the battle is between two 'wolves' inside us all. One is Evil. It is anger, envy, jealousy, sorrow, regret, greed, arrogance, self-pity, guilt, resentment, inferiority, lies, false pride, superiority and ego.

"The other is Good. It is joy, peace, love, hope, serenity, humility, kindness, benevolence, empathy, generosity, truth, compassion and faith."

The grandson thought about that for a minute, and then asked his grandfather, "Which wolf wins the fight?"

This popular parable is a reminder that we can control our thoughts and feelings—and release ourselves from our own prison. It doesn't matter if you've spent years and years feeding the evil wolf, even if you haven't been doing so consciously. All that matters now is that you open your eyes, open your heart, open your mind—and begin to grow your awareness, and start feeding the good wolf.

Right now, you can make a choice to no longer feed the thoughts within you that awaken fear, anxiety and stress.

Awareness is like a muscle—it becomes stronger the more you exercise and train it. If you practise awareness, you will soon be able to observe your thoughts as they emerge onto the screen of your mind. Once you can observe your thoughts, you have the power to rewrite your narrative and change your perception, and then change the emotional state that is attached to any event you have ever experienced, both in the present and in the past.

TAKE ACTION!
- Think of situations in your life where you are constantly fighting life.
- When do you experience a state of flow?
- What thoughts hold you prisoner in your own mind?

Chapter 4
Perception: How You Experience the World

There is no truth. There is only perception.
– Gustave Flaubert

You experience the world through your perception. It is the lens through which you view everything around you, and it dictates how you comprehend and attach meaning to events.

We each have our own unique perspective, based on what we've experienced and how we've understood those experiences. Sometimes two people may see things through a similar lens. At other times, you may have a completely different perception from someone who experienced the same event alongside you.

Think of pink or yellow lenses on a pair of sunglasses. When you look at any object through the pink lens, it looks pink. And when you look through the yellow lens, everything takes on a yellow hue. A hugely powerful human realisation is that—just as you can take off and put on a pair of tinted sunglasses you can learn to control how you perceive an event. With practice, you can even go back and reassess past events, and see how it feels to look at them through a different pair of lenses, a different tint.

This is how you experience things[3]:

1. An event takes place. You have no control over it because it happens outside of you.
2. Through the lens of your perception, you observe the event and interpret what it means. A single event can have many different interpretations; you usually choose what feels most congruent to you in that moment. Often, your interpretation is shaped by your current mood—are you happy, tired, grumpy, relaxed, angry, in a rush? Your interpretation becomes a story about the event and what it means to you. In this process, you apply a set of labels and thoughts to the event.
3. The thoughts created by your story trigger corresponding feelings that carry an emotional charge. Your thoughts may make you feel indifferent (neutral), good (positive) or bad (negative). You may label what is happening as being right or wrong. If you have labelled the event as right or good, you might feel happy or excited. If you have labelled it as wrong or bad, you may feel sad or angry.
4. Your thoughts and feelings, based on your perceived interpretation of the event, will now dictate the action you take. Maybe you do nothing, or maybe you take action that is either empowered or disempowered.

This entire cycle plays out subconsciously after every single event or situation and creates your experience.

It's important to realise that as much as you would love it, you have no control over the actual events that take place in your life. When you leave home in the morning, you have no control over the amount of traffic on the road or the car that cuts you off. You cannot control whether one of your clients will cancel an order, whether a critical co-worker will be sick, whether a friend or family member will say something you don't like, or whether there'll be a queue for the treadmill at the gym. This is all out of your control.

Thinking that you can control external events creates immense suffering— it's an example of trying to fight life, trying to fight the universe. Fighting life is absolutely exhausting and is not something I would recommend. I've tried it!

But there is some good news.

> "Just as thoughts are the language of the brain, feelings are the language of the body. And how you think and how you feel create a state of being. A state of being is when your mind and body are working together."
>
> – Dr Joe Dispenza

We've agreed you have no control over the event. But you do have 100% control over your perception and interpretation of the event. By choosing your interpretation, you can change what an event means to you, triggering a different set of thoughts and feelings that will empower what action you take.

So you do have control! Not of the event, but of the cycle that takes place between the event and you taking action.

If you grasp this concept, you will gain tremendous power. This is what mindset mastery is all about: switching from automatic reactions to responses that you consciously choose and control.

Here's a scenario. You have a meeting scheduled with your biggest client and your boss. Thinking ahead, you leave for the office with time to spare, but as you turn onto the main road, you see the most horrific traffic. All of a sudden, thoughts are firing through your brain, many of them, as Robert Greene says, irrational. You start to create a narrative for the situation: Why me? I always have the worst luck. I'm going to be so late. Life is so unfair. I hope I don't get fired… Doom and gloom.

When you think that "Life is so unfair," you trigger undesirable feelings like anger, stress and anxiety. These feelings go on to create your state of being. Your journey to the office becomes unpleasant. You cut into gaps, you speed, you drive recklessly—all while playing through the worst-case scenarios of what your boss is going to do.

And it doesn't stop there, because your state of mind lasts well after the original thoughts have died down. You arrive at work, snap at a co-worker and remain angry the whole day. When you get home, you kick your dog and scream at your kids.

Get where I'm going with this? It started with a bit of traffic, which snowballed into an avalanche of pain.

So let's think how the same situation could have been interpreted for a more positive and empowering outcome. Let's say that as you turn out onto the main road, you realise that the traffic (the event) is completely out of your control. Instead of allowing your thoughts to run away from you, you consciously let go and flow with the moment. You think about the positive aspects of the situation. You now have some extra time to listen to that awesome podcast you've downloaded, which may help you better approach the work that lies ahead of you today. Or you choose to spend the time thinking through the challenge your client is facing. When you do get to the office, you discover that your client and boss were both stuck in the same traffic jam—and you all arrive together. Your client is flustered but you manage to calm the situation with some good humour. You're able to add good value to the meeting and take your upbeat energy into the rest of your day, having a positive impact on everyone around you.

Can you see how the same event that triggered anger and anxiety in the first scenario could also be an opportunity to feel a sense of gratitude, peace and calm? You get to decide the lens through which you view any event.

Which scenario would you choose?

Every event is neutral. The only meaning it has is the meaning you attach to it. No-one else attaches the meaning for you. It's an inside job—one you can use to create a sense of harmony and flow in your life.

TAKE ACTION!
- What events or situations trigger an instant negative reaction in you?
- Are there specific people who tend to trigger you more?
- How would it affect your state if you no longer reacted to these events and people?

Chapter 5
Feeding an Empowering or Disempowering Cycle

We've just looked at perception, and how you create your experience in the world and ultimately your reality. Now let's look at a cycle that is set in motion by your beliefs, and how this affects the actions you take.

Beliefs are incredibly powerful—it is your beliefs and their associated thoughts that create your feelings, which drive your actions and in turn create the results you see in your life. Your results support your beliefs, and the cycle continues.

This cycle can either empower you or disempower you.

Let's see how this cycle can play out in two completely different ways.

Imagine you've just been employed as a salesperson. If you fundamentally believe that you're no good at sales and you keep thinking you're going to fail, you will create feelings of fear and anxiety. You won't feel confident in your job. You won't feel inspired or motivated. This in turn will lead to poor performance and you won't get good results, which will further reinforce your belief that you're a bad salesperson. Your negative belief intensifies with each cycle. Soon you believe you're a terrible salesperson. After a few cycles, you believe you're a horrific salesperson and feel completely useless.

Or: from the outset you believe you're a great salesperson. Your belief creates feelings of excitement and confidence. Empowered by your beliefs and feelings, you perform well and get the great results you thought you could—you shoot the lights out and exceed your target. These amazing results strengthen your belief that you really are a great salesperson. Your positive belief intensifies with each cycle. After a few cycles, you feel completely confident—you love the product, and the job feels easy.

And where does this all start? Yes—with your thoughts and beliefs.

You have the power to decide whether you disempower yourself by assuming the worst, or whether you learn to take control of your thoughts so you can consciously choose an empowered approach.

Let's explore the power of this idea in more detail by imagining something seemingly inconsequential.

You're driving along and there's a small gap in front of you. As you near a red traffic light, a car suddenly cuts into the gap from the lane next to you. You're forced to slam on the brakes to avoid bashing into them.

A DISEMPOWERING NARRATIVE

Adrenaline shoots through your body, increasing your heart rate and your breathing. Reactively, you blow up in anger: "You idiot! Didn't you see me? What's wrong with you?" You curse and throw zap signs through the window.

That small incident holds you captive: your angry mood affects your morning, and you go through the day being reactive and feeling like crap.

Can you see how you become a slave to your thoughts and feelings in this narrative? Now, let's rewrite the story so you experience an empowering cycle— so that, no matter what happens, nothing can affect your flow.

AN EMPOWERING NARRATIVE

As the car cuts you off, you're forced to slam on your brakes, which triggers the release of adrenaline. But instead of reacting, you've taught yourself to take a moment, pause and assess the situation. You recognise that you're about to get swept away in anger.

In this moment of conscious awareness (the pause), you have created a gap between the event and your reaction. Now, instead of automatically assuming the worst, you can imagine a narrative that will support a healthier response. Your new thoughts could look something like this:

Maybe this person is experiencing a crisis and needs to get somewhere far more urgently than I do.

Maybe he's really late for work...

Maybe her child has just had an accident at school... Maybe her parent is being rushed to hospital...

You are choosing a narrative and a perspective that fuels an empowering narrative, you can imagine that this person may be in a serious situation themselves. You could even be grateful that you're not in the same position, and you could send them a silent blessing for whatever they may be dealing with.

Instead of feeling anger, you've chosen a state of love, compassion, empathy and even grace.

Remember that you are doing this for yourself, not for the other person. You're not shifting your perspective for anyone other than yourself. They aren't even aware that their actions have triggered the cycle that's playing out in your reality—whether empowering or disempowering—and that's totally fine.

You are choosing a narrative and a perspective that fuels a positive, empowered feeling and outcome. You are choosing to empower yourself no matter what transpires. You are controlling the quality of your thoughts, which dictate your feelings, which create your state. You are thus consciously creating a stable state of calm, peace and serenity—a state where you can respond in a healthy manner instead of needing to react.

This is Ownership 101: owning your thoughts and feelings, becoming the master of how you think and feel. This is a powerful place from which to create, because no-one other than you can determine your state or push you out of flow.

Chapter 6
Shifting Your Perspective

We are, as a species, addicted to story.
Even when the body goes to sleep, the mind stays up all night, telling itself
stories.
– Jonathan Gottschall

"Tell me a story": four incredibly powerful words, and a means by which humans have shared their legacy and history throughout the ages.

There is something so magical and captivating about storytelling. Stories have the power to transport you—you can be at home watching a movie, but a romance can have you swooning in the arms of a lover, while a fast-paced thriller can have you on the edge of your seat, nerves shredded and adrenaline pumping. Stories trigger thoughts, thoughts trigger the corresponding feelings, and your thoughts and feelings together empower or disempower your actions.

Did you know that when it comes to your life, you are the master storyteller?

You are the author of your own life. You hold the pen.

It is up to you not only to craft the story yet to be written, but also to go back and edit the previous chapters. By reshaping the way you tell your story, you can redefine the beliefs, thoughts and feelings you have attached to it—no matter when the actual events happened.

Of course you cannot go back in time and physically relive an event. But by going back and sifting through your thoughts, your perception of any event can be reworked, and you can change what it means to you as many times as you like. This is how you can shift from a disempowered narrative that keeps you stuck to an empowered one that positively drives you forward. In the new story, you can rewrite your role as the hero and not the victim.

Anxiety is a feeling that is triggered when you feel like you don't have any options. Feeling that you have limited options can be caused by the belief that you aren't in control of your own story, that someone else is sitting at the typewriter, crafting the narrative of your life.

But this isn't true. The person creating your story is you.

How many times have you've heard someone say, "You made me angry" or "You make me sad"? The truth is, no-one can make you feel anything without your permission. They can act in a certain way, say certain things, but you alone decide how to process and respond to them.

The only person who can attach what anything means to you is you.

Grammy Award-winning choir director Kirk Franklin provides the following beautiful story that illustrates how two people experiencing the same event can interpret it in completely different ways.

THE TWINS[4]

Twin boys were raised by an alcoholic father.

One grew up to be an alcoholic. When asked what happened, he said, "I watched my father."

The other grew up and never drank in his life. When asked what happened, he said, "I watched my father."

Two boys, same dad, two different perspectives. Your perspective in life will determine your destination.

Their perspective is what makes them bitter, or better.

Another story that illustrates our choice to see an event through the lens of good or bad is the fable of the farmer.

THE FARMER'S FABLE[5]

One day, a farmer's only horse ran away.

His neighbours came over to console him, saying, "We're so very sorry, this is horrible news! You must feel angry and sad."

The farmer said, "We'll see. Who can know what is good and what is bad?"

The next week, the farmer's horse returned, with a dozen wild horses following behind. The farmer and his son rounded up the horses.

His neighbours came over, and this time they said, "Wow, what good fortune! How joyful you must feel!"

Again, the farmer said, "We shall see. Who can know what is good and what is bad?"

The following day, one of the new wild horses trampled the farmer's son, breaking his legs.

The neighbours then said, "We're so sorry for you. You must be upset with this terrible happening."

The farmer replied, "We shall see. Who can know what is good and what is bad?"

Shortly thereafter, the country went to war, and every healthy young man was drafted to fight. Due to his injuries, the farmer's son was not drafted.

It was a horrible war. Many soldiers died.

The farmer's neighbours congratulated him, saying,

"You must be so happy and relieved that your son did not go to war!"

What did the farmer reply?

"We shall see. Who can know what is good and what is bad?

I need to repeat the critical point here: every event in life is actually neutral— we attach the meaning.

> "There is nothing either good or bad, but thinking makes it so."
> – Hamlet

We like to label events, when in truth every situation just is. It is through the lens of our perception that an event becomes something.

The beautiful thing about a label is that if you don't like it, you can scratch it off and apply another. Shifting perspective is a superpower you always have at the ready, one that can transform your state of mind and attachment to any event, circumstance or situation.

TAKE ACTION!

Write down a list of prominent events that have shaped your life, then label which you think are "good" and which are "bad".

- Why do you feel that way about them? What meaning have you attached to the event?
- Has this thinking created empowering or disempowering cycles for you?
- What would it be like if the events were neither good nor bad, but just events?

Chapter 7
The Power Is in the Pause

Between stimulus and response, there is a space.
In that space lies our freedom and our power
to choose our response. In our response
lies our growth and our happiness.
– Alex Pattakos

The ability to create a pause before you react to any life situation is what truly creates freedom. When you can consciously respond to life's events in ways that serve you, you are no longer a prisoner of your own mind. You become free to make empowering choices that set you up for success.

The magic happens in the pause.

It is the pause that gives you space to breathe. This allows the sensory signals from the event to move from your reptilian centre—the basal ganglia that just want to fight, flee or freeze—to your frontal lobe, where rational thinking can kick in.

TAKE ACTION!
- How reactive are you?
- How often during the course of a day do you feel that you react to events and situations without any thought (faster than Usain Bolt out the blocks during a 100-metre sprint)?

Mel Robbins, author of *The 5 Second Rule*, has a process for beginning a task: she first counts backwards from five, like they do when a rocket launches.

When she reaches "one", she starts the activity—this way, she doesn't give her brain time to become distracted or to talk her out of starting.

> "You can't control how you feel. But you can always choose how you act."
> – Mel Robbins

The same rule can be used to shift from "reaction" to "response": counting from one to five, or backwards from five to one, will create the space you need to choose a thought-out response over an involuntary reaction.

In this pause, it's important to breathe. When we are triggered, adrenaline and other chemicals shoot through our body, and we tend to hold our breath, which just creates more tension and anxiety.

You can use the pause to create space to ask yourself quality questions that will determine the outcome you're after. If you're triggered by an event, you can ask yourself:

Why am I feeling this way?
Is this a trigger from my past?
Who do I want to be in this moment?

Many refer to this space or pause as mindfulness. Mindfulness is about coming back to yourself, becoming centred, and empowering yourself to respond from a place of consideration and intention. I like the term "purposeful intent": when you do something

> "The quality of your life is a direct reflection of the quality of the questions you are asking yourself."
> – Tony Robbins

with purposeful intent, you know exactly what outcome you are trying to create (the purpose) in any given situation, and you are less likely to be swept away by tumultuous thoughts and feelings.

Looking back on my life, I've found that most of the mess I created was the result of being swept away in momentary thoughts and feelings that created negative or destructive reactions and outcomes. That's why learning how to

> "If you don't learn to control your thoughts, you will never learn how to control your behaviour."
> – Joyce Meyer

control our thoughts, feelings and responses in life is a superpower.

Here's what the process of shifting your narrative looks like, step by step:

- Become aware that you are being triggered to react automatically to an event.
- Pause to create space to think with purposeful intent.
- Decide not to react.
- Replace your internal story with a more empowering one.
- Respond from a place of peace and calm.

TAKE ACTION!
- Think of situations or events that trigger automatic reactions for you.
- In the moment, what is your predominant thought and feeling attached to the event?
- How can you shift the narrative to create a more empowered response?

Chapter 8
The Perfect Experience

During the four months I spent in a drug-rehab centre, we would start every morning with an hour's session with a spiritual guru. Don Tait, a man in his seventies, had been a hotshot litigation attorney in Canada until drugs and alcohol destroyed his life. He'd since dedicated himself to helping recovering alcoholics and addicts. I thought he was fascinating, and I found the wisdom he shared with us each morning to be invaluable. He shared freely; nothing was taboo. There were so many stories from his battle with drugs and alcohol that I could relate to.

There was one message in particular that stood out for me, one sentence he repeated almost every single day: "No matter what you have been through, it was, is and will always be the perfect experience you needed to have."

It helped me realise that every single experience has a purpose; everything that happens is exactly what we need to awaken and grow. There is a hidden blessing and a lesson in every situation—we just need to learn how to look for it.

This was such a powerful concept to me. I looked back to the events through my life during which I'd experienced the most pain. Slowly I began to see that each one carried a blessing and a lesson.

I'd always wished for a more present father figure, but if I'd had one, I wouldn't have grown into the independent man I am today—I had to figure things out for myself. I'd wished that my family's finances were better, but if they had been, I wouldn't have earned my own pocket money from a young age—which helped me learn about money. I'd desperately wanted to study after I left high school, but if I had, I wouldn't have built businesses in the media and advertising space—businesses that set me up for real success in the property industry once I'd turned my life around.

Every situation that I'd thought was there to break me actually made me into the person I am today. What I'd seen as setbacks were actually setups that had catapulted me towards my purpose better than if things had worked out the way I'd envisaged.

In my active alcoholism and addiction, I was constantly fighting life. I'd often find myself thinking, This shouldn't be happening to me. When things didn't go according to my plan, I would fight, force and push with all my might. And this was the root of a lot of my suffering.

In one of his workshops, Tony Robbins spoke to a man in the audience. The man told Tony he was suffering because his mother had recently died. Tony's reply was brutal and straightforward. He said, "You are not suffering because your mother died. You are suffering because you think she shouldn't have."

You suffer when you hold on to the idea that you shouldn't be going through an experience. Suffering is created by your resistance to reality, to truth.

It's the fight that creates the suffering. You bitterly hold on to the idea of how you want a situation or event to unfold, rejecting the reality of what's transpiring. This causes internal conflict and awakens emotions of sadness, anxiety, stress, anger, resentment, guilt, shame and even jealousy.

Imagine embracing the idea that every single event, every experience, has been placed in your path to make you, not to break you.

A great example—one we've all probably experienced—is a breakup with a romantic partner. When you're going through a breakup, it feels devastating. You're sad and frustrated, and sometimes you can't imagine your life without that person who's now lost to you. Time passes, and at some point you meet someone new. All of a sudden, you find yourself in love with this new person. The previous heartbreak has become a distant memory; the old has made room for the new.

There was purpose in the breakup, purpose in the pain. It wasn't a setback—it was a setup for a new season.

THE SUCCESSIVE FAILURES OF JACK MA

Jack Ma is a Chinese businessman who went through a lot of rejection in his early years—but he didn't let that stop him. He failed a key primary-school test twice. He failed in middle school three times. He failed three years at university. He wanted to be a policeman, but was rejected because they thought he was too weak. He has described how he applied for 30 jobs and got rejected every time. When KFC launched in China, he was one of 24 businessmen to apply for a licence to run an outlet—and he was the only one who was rejected. He applied to Harvard, not once, not twice, but 10 times, and every time he was turned down.

Finally, Jack Ma raised capital for and founded an online wholesale portal called Alibaba. As Alibaba's executive chairman, he steered the company to incredible success. It went public in 2014 and became one of the biggest companies in the world, its value rising to $850-billion in 2020—not bad for someone who had to endure successive failures and rejections.

Now, what would've happened if Jack Ma been awarded a KFC licence, or got into Harvard? He may have become a wealthy man selling fried chicken, or may have been stuck working a corporate job as a consultant. Who knows—but his life would have looked very different from the way it does right now.

At the time of writing, Alibaba faced regulatory headwinds in China, and Jack Ma's personal net worth had dropped to "only" around $40-billion—but with an attitude like his, you can bet he'll come out just fine.

Jack Ma went through the perfect experience to take him where he is now—and you are doing that too. You may not want to believe it, or you may not see it right at this moment, but give it some time and you will look back and marvel how every single twist and turn in your plot held purpose. The key is to stop resisting what is unfolding in your life.

Don't fight it, and don't stop going.

LATE FOR WORK

Here's a tale I've adapted from a number of similar stories I've come across.

James, an overachieving New York stockbroker, came downstairs for breakfast at 6.45am, as he always did. He wanted to get to work by 8am to catch up on some urgent calls before his usual 9am status meeting. At the breakfast table, he was enjoying his regular morning chat with his daughter when she leaned over to show him a picture she'd drawn—and accidentally spilled his full cup of coffee onto his smart grey trousers. Startled by the hot coffee pouring onto his lap, James dashed upstairs to change his pants. It was just past 7am, and he had an hour's commute to get into the city centre.

James hurried down the stairs, kissed his daughter on the forehead, hugged his wife and headed out the front door. As he dashed across the porch, his Labrador, Timmy, bolted out from nowhere and ran through James's legs, excited to greet the postman who at that moment was walking past. Since Timmy was a bit on the heavy side, James lost his balance and fell down two porch steps onto the grass that had just been watered.

James was now getting frustrated—his shirt and pants were marked with soil. Picking himself up, he darted inside and upstairs to change for the second time.

At 7.08am, he finally jumped into his car and sped off down the road, thinking, I've got so much to do today. I'm never going to get through my backlog. His anxiety worsened as he turned onto the freeway into bumper-to-bumper traffic. James swore and his blood began to boil. "Why me?" he shouted at the clear blue sky.

At 8.36am, James crossed the Brooklyn Bridge to get into Manhattan. But there was a broken-down truck in one of the lanes, and a bottleneck as the cars ahead of him were diverted into a single lane. James was furious, wondering why he always had such bad luck.

"What else could possibly go wrong this morning?" he muttered to himself.

By 8.46am, he was finally just a few streets away from the office.

But as he headed down the road leading straight to his building, he heard a loud rumbling. Peering through his windscreen in the direction of the deafening noise, he watched in shock as a low-flying plane came hurtling over his car, and crashed into the office block in front of him.

The day was September 11, 2001. James's office was on the 95th floor of the North Tower at the World Trade Center—the site of the first crash.[6]

If James had arrived at the office just five minutes earlier, he would've been dead. He would never have seen his wife, his artistic daughter or his clumsy Labrador ever again. In a single moment, the meaning of that morning's delays changed for James. The events that had pushed him into an anxious, angry rage had become his greatest gift and blessing, and allowed him to live another day.

The point is that every experience is the perfect experience you need to have in order to grow and wake up. Not just some events—all of them.

When you stop fighting life and instead seek the lesson in every event, you welcome a state of flow into your life. Letting go of the need to fight life frees you from the captivity of your mind. In a flow state, you can create. Nothing outside of you, no event or situation, is able to upset the internal state you've chosen, and you will be calm and at peace.

So, can you please stop fighting life? Let go and let it flow.

TAKE ACTION!
- Can you relate to James in the story you've just read?
  Have there been times in your life when you've become irritated, frustrated and annoyed, only to find out later that you'd been protected?
- Think of past situations that have upset you, but that in hindsight you recognise as blessings.
- What events do you wish had not taken place?
- How did you feel at the time?
- Can you think of ways in which these events served you?

Chapter 9
Growth Happens in Dark Places

————————

Life isn't just about darkness or light.
Rather it's about finding light within the darkness.
— Landon Parham

————————

When I think back over the trouble I created in my life during my years of alcoholism and addiction, I can now see that my greatest growth happened in the darkest times.

My character was crafted when I felt utterly helpless and hopeless. It was during moments of sheer despair, when I thought I wouldn't make it through, that I proved to myself that I could. I couldn't see it then, but looking back, I feel only gratitude for the times I felt my worst, because they drove me to seek change. I'm sure you've also felt loss and despair in your life. You've also had no idea how you're going to make it. The world has felt dark and heavy on your shoulders. The truth is, if you're reading this book right now, you have made it through. And I want to remind you that if you ever feel that way again, you'll make it through again.

I look back at my life with a deep knowing that no matter what I face in the future, absolutely nothing can keep me stuck again. Through the mountains of pain, the challenges and the obstacles, I have taught myself time and time again that I can and will bounce back.

If you take a jar of seeds and put them on a shelf, what happens? Well, nothing—that's not what seeds are for. But when you take a seed and press it into moist soil, engulf it in darkness, that

"They tried to bury us. They didn't know we were seeds."
— Mexican proverb

is when the roots begin to delve into the ground and later shoots spring forth, breaking through the surface towards the light.

Think of yourself as a seed. Without the dark, you cannot fulfil your purpose, and your value cannot be unlocked.

> "Grapes must be crushed to make wine. Diamonds form under pressure. Olives are pressed to release oil. Seeds grow in darkness. Whenever you feel crushed, under pressure, pressed, or in darkness, you're in a powerful place of transformation and transmutation. Trust the process."
>
> – Lalah Delia

If you are alive and breathing, then it is an absolute truth that you will face pain, obstacles and challenges. It never stops. This is how we grow.

When you feel crushed, under pressure, pressed upon or in darkness, you are faced with two options: you can give up (which I don't recommend), or you can show up for yourself and rise above the situation, growing character and resilience in the process. To rise above means that you have to learn something new: to get OVA the challenge ahead, you have to dig deep.

The beautiful thing is that once you get over the pain, obstacle or challenge, you'll have new tools and skills, so that next time things will be easier.

> "It's always darkest just before dawn."
>
> – Thomas Fuller

If you feel like your life is currently in darkness, prepare yourself: you're about to have the greatest breakthrough.

So don't be afraid of the dark.

TAKE ACTION!
- What have been the darkest moments, or most painful events, challenges and obstacles in your life?
- When you think about those times, how do you feel?
- Do you think the feelings you've attached to the events serve you – or do they keep you stuck?

Chapter 10
There Is Purpose in Pain

Without pain, there would be no suffering; without suffering, we would never learn from our mistakes. To make it right, pain and suffering are the key to all windows; without it, there is no way of life.
– Angelina Jolie

Imagine for a moment that you touch a hot stove. As you feel the heat, you immediately pull your hand away. This is the main purpose of pain—to motivate you into action. Sometimes your reaction is instant, as with the hot stove; at other times, the pain has to increase before you finally take action.

Maybe you're stuck in a comfort zone. Maybe you've been procrastinating about following up on an idea. Maybe you're delaying a business you want to launch. Maybe you feel stuck in a job you hate or a relationship that isn't serving you.

> "Pain makes me grow. Growing is what I want. Therefore, for me pain is pleasure."
> – Arnold Schwarzenegger

I can almost guarantee that if you haven't trained yourself to be self-motivated and self-disciplined, you might not take action until something painful happens that forces you to move.

When I was 25, I was grossly overweight, weighing in at nearly 100 kilograms. I had a triple chin and really hated the body I was in. I had a beautiful girlfriend, but she wouldn't be physical with me and wouldn't even hold my hand in public.

One night I had a run-in with an ex-boyfriend of hers, and he said, "Why would a girl like that want to be seen with a guy like you?"

It was painful to hear him say that, but it was the truth. I didn't respect my body. Endless nights of cocaine and alcohol binges followed by comfort-eating hadn't done my physique any good.

When I went home that night, I looked in the mirror and said, "He's right. Why would she want to be seen in public with me?"

I remember the moment so clearly.

Instead of playing the victim and getting angry with him, I was pushed into action by the pain of his words. And boy, did I take action: the next week I hired a personal trainer and immediately got on a healthy diet plan. No longer did I wolf down half a kilogram of pasta with butter and sweet-chilli sauce at 3am when I came home from a club. I started training three evenings a week with my trainer, and the other days I trained by myself. I woke up super-early every day for cardio. I became obsessed with the process as I saw my body and my relationship with it start to transform.

Within eight months I'd lost 28 kilograms, and I felt amazing. Within a year, my physical transformation had collected a number of accolades. In 2010, I was selected as a CLEO "Most Eligible Bachelor", nominated as one of GQ's "Top 10 Best Dressed Men" and made it to the semi-finals of Mr South Africa. I was still with the same girlfriend—who now had no problem with public displays of affection!

The point is, I could have chosen to be a victim, and continued my cycle of self-pity and self-sabotage. But I had harnessed the power of pain and transformed that energy into something positive. I still had a long way to go in my transformative journey, but that was an invaluable lesson in itself, one of my first early steps.

There are so many examples of pain pushing people to take positive action. You might be stuck in a destructive relationship, but because you don't want to be alone, you stay—until the pain becomes unbearable. Whether it's through abuse, betrayal or cheating, it's pain that eventually makes you find the courage to walk away.

Or you may be stuck in a dead-end job that you hate. You're not aligned with the company's purpose and you still struggle each month to make ends meet. It may take a run-in with the boss to make you realise that enough is enough.

In that moment, charged with energy from the pain, you take the first steps towards positive change. If you can continue with the same

"Turn your wounds into wisdom."
                – Oprah Winfrey

momentum, your life will start moving in a positive direction. Even more than that, you will have been given the gift of being able to help someone else. If you've managed to get through a painful situation, you've equipped yourself with knowledge, tools and experience.

You now have a blessing and a responsibility: the blessing is that you can relate to someone who's as stuck as you once were—and the responsibility is to help them. Helping others is often just about being vulnerable, honest and open with your story. Serving others is part of your greatest purpose—something I will cover later in the book.

For me, the pain of alcoholism and addiction transformed into my new purpose of helping others. If I'd never felt stuck, I wouldn't have learnt how to get unstuck—and now I can share that lesson.

When I work out with my personal trainer, he pushes me past my pain barrier. He explains that it is the most painful reps that most effectively build muscle growth. If I'm not sore after my session, I'm a bit disappointed because I know I've wasted an opportunity to push myself to my limits.

Pain has become my friend. I wake up every morning and I say, "Bring it on." I welcome pain, obstacles and challenges because I want to be stretched, I want to grow, I want to be the best version of myself that I can possibly be.

Because I hold the belief that I will grow the most through pain, challenges and obstacles, I seek them out.

I can find pleasure in the pain.

> "Out of suffering have emerged the strongest souls; the most massive characters are seared with scars."
>
> – Kahlil Gibran

Chapter 11
Attachment to Pain

———————

The root of all suffering is attachment.
– Buddha

———————

It may surprise you to know that our attachment to past pain is often greater than the pain itself: the story we tell of pain we've endured has become such a big part of our identity that we don't want to let that story go. You repeat your story and maybe people feel sorry for you; they empathise, and it's through holding on to the pain that you experience connection. Maybe you've told the story so many times that you've anchored your very existence to a painful experience—the story of your pain is who you are.

What I need to ask is this: how is that story serving you?

The only reason we hold on to anything in our life is because we believe there's a positive payoff. If we know it isn't serving us, then it should be easy to let go. So the key question is, if the attachment to pain is keeping you stuck and you're constantly creating suffering in your mind, could you consider letting go of the pain?

An anchor keeps a ship from moving away. It's the same when you anchor yourself to your story of pain: you feel stuck. The story prevents you from moving forward, it disempowers you, it robs you of vital energy and the excitement needed to step forward into your future.

In order to experience growth and progress, you have to lift the anchor (your attachment) to the painful memories of the past. You have to be prepared to let go of the story. The thought of letting go of the story often seems even more painful than the experience itself, so you cling for dear life to a narrative that has shaped you, given you a reason to blame others, and been an excuse for why you're not taking any positive action.

Here's the thing: you can have a breakthrough or you can make excuses—you cannot do both.

The time has come to break free, to reprogramme the narrative and your relationship with the events that keep you anchored to the pain.

TAKE ACTION!
- What painful stories have you attached to your identity?
- How do these stories serve you?
- What would happen if you let go of these stories?

Chapter 12
Taking 100% Responsibility

You cannot control what happens to you, but you can control your attitude towards what happens to you —and in that, you will be mastering change rather than allowing it to master you.

– Brian Tracy

I hope by now it is clear that you and you alone are 100% responsible for your thoughts and feelings.

No-one can make you angry, sad, depressed or anxious. A person can act in a certain way that you may not like or agree with, but you are the author of the narrative that you attach to their actions. Only you can decide on the feelings other people's actions will trigger in you. No-one can make you feel anything without your implicit permission, because you have allowed your thoughts to form a disempowering narrative.

This goes for any situation. You are always in full control of how you think, feel and act, and there is not a single situation in which you lose that control— unless you allow it. The only time you don't have control is when you slip into your conditioned, automatic patterns and reactions.

When I was an alcoholic, I would blame my parents. I'd say, "Well, they did drugs. When they fought, they'd get aggressive. I'm like this because of them. It's just who I am." With this, I gave away all my power and justified my behaviour— which kept me stuck.

"You, and only you, are ultimately responsible for who you become and how happy you are."

– Rachel Hollis

If you blame, complain or accuse another person of making you feel a certain way, you've given them all your power. But when you change the narrative, you change the feeling.

As with everything in life, with practice comes progress and eventually mastery. When you first begin the process of controlling your narrative, you find your thoughts racing all over the place. But with time and conscious practice, it gets easier and easier to choose a narrative that empowers positive action. Eventually it becomes second nature, a natural unconscious habit. It's worth noting that the same rule applies when you make someone else responsible for your happiness. It is doomed to failure because you have no control over that person's thoughts, feelings or actions. You cannot determine how they will behave or treat you. When you give them the responsibility of making you happy, you give away the power to decide your own level of happiness—which is a fast track to disappointment and suffering.

Taking back your power and committing to being 100% responsible for your thoughts, feelings, actions and overall state makes you unstoppable and empowered as you move towards your goals and dreams.

TAKE ACTION!
- Do you find that you make excuses for your behaviour?
- Do you blame others?
- Who do you blame for where you find yourself in life today?
- How inspired do you feel to take action when you are blaming, complaining or making excuses?
- Could you decide to let go of this disempowering narrative?

Chapter 13
Acceptance and Surrender

The moment that judgment stops through acceptance of what is, you are free of the mind. You have made room for love, for joy, for peace.

– Eckhart Tolle

Two powerful concepts I learnt in rehab changed my life forever. They are acceptance and surrender.

Acceptance is embracing the reality of an event, situation or circumstance. This doesn't mean you have to like or even condone what is going on. You just have to acknowledge that it is happening and that you are powerless to change it, and to be aware of the thoughts and feelings that are awakened.

When something happens that you don't like or things don't go your way, your natural reaction is to reject what is happening. You don't want to believe that this is the reality you are facing, and this resistance creates suffering: you create stress, anxiety and frustration as you fight against the reality of what is.

Always say "yes" to the present moment. What could be more futile, more insane, than to create inner resistance to what already is? What could be more insane than to oppose life itself, which is now and always now? Surrender to what is. Say "yes" to life—and see how life suddenly starts working for you rather than against you.

– Eckhart Tolle

Acceptance is the practised discipline of letting go of your resistance to what has happened in the past and what is happening in the present moment. It is simply acknowledging what is happening, and giving it permission to be, without fighting against it or rejecting it.

"It is what it is"—this simple sentence distils the concept of acceptance.

In the beginning, acceptance is hard. I didn't want to accept the hand I'd been dealt in my life, so I would constantly fight and push back. *Why is this happening to me? What have I done to deserve this? Why is life out to get me?* This was so draining and took tremendous amounts of energy—energy that could've been better used to find solutions.

But, like any new discipline, acceptance can be practised, even on the smallest scale.

You get up in the morning and there's no hot water. Instead of getting angry, embrace the reality that you have no control over the situation, and transform the narrative. Maybe you pretend you're in the wild and have to take a cold shower before embarking on your epic quest in the concrete jungle...

> "God grant me the serenity to accept the things I cannot change, the courage to change the things I can, and the wisdom to know the difference."
>
> – Serenity prayer

Or, next time you're delayed when running late, let go of the initial feeling of frustration. Call the person you're on your way to and let them know that you're terribly sorry but you will be a bit late. Then put on your favourite music and jam in the car.

When you come home and your partner snaps at you, instead of assuming it's all about you, embrace compassion. Maybe they've had a tough day. Accept that you cannot change what has happened to them or how they've spoken to you, but know that you have 100% control over how you interpret the event, and that you are responsible for creating a more empowered response. Switch from a fear-based response (lashing out) to one of love—defuse the situation by wrapping them in a massive hug and telling them everything's going to be okay.

Acceptance is not an excuse to give up, or to not grow, change or take action. It's not saying, "Oh well, this is how it is. I can't do anything about it."

Practising acceptance means withdrawing your resistance so you have more energy to change and move forward. You can accept that, right now, you don't feel good in your body—but you can still take action by starting a balanced diet and getting your ass to the gym. You can accept that some of your behaviours are destructive while you craft a plan to address them and change. You can accept that you have a difficult relationship with your father, sister or child, but you can still find the courage to work on it and improve it over time.

Accepting a situation also doesn't mean that it will stay that way forever. We overestimate what we can achieve in a year, and grossly underestimate what we can achieve in a decade. When I think back to my active addiction, I recall that I hated the man I was. Today I see my value and worth. I treat myself with love and kindness, and have a completely different relationship with myself. Had you told me then that I'd get to the place I am today, I would have laughed at you. Things can change, and they do.

On your journey of growth, acceptance will smooth the path and remove resistance, anxiety and stress so you can focus on crafting your vision and taking action towards your goals.

Surrender is the award-winning support act for acceptance. Surrender is about giving up the fight. It's about submitting to life and knowing that even if you do everything right, situations will arise that do not align with your desired direction or outcome.

Whether you believe in the universe, God, Mother Nature or anything else, surrender is about knowing there is an order to things. For me, surrender comes with knowing that no matter what happens, I am divinely taken care of and there is a purpose to every season. When I surrender, I let go. In that powerful moment, I release the need to control the things around me, and I find my ultimate state of *flow*.

There is so much strength in surrender.

Surrender is not about giving up your own power—it's about acknowledging your human limitations and embracing the all-encompassing creative life force of the universe.

"Surrender is a journey from the outer turmoil to the inner peace."
— Sri Chinmoy

TAKE ACTION!
- When you think of acceptance and surrender, what do you feel?
- Where do you battle to accept an event or situation in your life?
- How could surrender improve your internal state of being?

Chapter 14
Letting Go of Toxic Emotions

I don't want to be at the mercy of my emotions.
I want to use them, to enjoy them,
and to dominate them.
– Oscar Wilde

It's been scientifically proven that some emotions are heavier than others. When you feel an emotion, your body releases hormones: oxytocin when you are happy, and adrenaline, noradrenaline and cortisol when you are angry. Interestingly, these stress hormones are literally four times heavier in weight than oxytocin!

Still, it's important to realise that there's no such thing as a "bad" emotion. All emotions serve a purpose, even the uncomfortable ones.

Emotions are triggers that indicate where you need kindness, gentleness, healing and growth in yourself. Problem is, we often don't deal with these emotions when they surface. Why? Because we don't know how to process them in a healthy way. We lack the understanding or the tools to work through them.

"Your emotions are the slaves to your thoughts, and you are the slave to your emotions."

– Elizabeth Gilbert

Many of us have been taught that negative emotions are "bad" or that they make us "weak". Instead of accepting how we are feeling and dealing with it, we bury the emotion. But running and hiding from it only makes it grow bigger.

Holding on to anger and resentment will make you an angry, resentful person who lashes out at those around you. Bottled-up emotions have a tendency to burst out and can end up hurting those who haven't even hurt you. Maybe you've seen the meme that says: "If you don't heal what hurt you, you'll bleed on people who didn't cut you."

Guilt and shame both have the prolonged effects of making you feel undeserving, less than, not enough or unworthy. On a subconscious level you feel undeserving of love or success, so you beat yourself up and sabotage your opportunities and relationships—anything that feels too good to be true.

As you can see, when we don't deal with these emotions, they wreak havoc in our lives, adding drama, admin, stress and anxiety. While they can prompt us to change our lives for the better, it's when we hold on to them and use them as an anchor that they become toxic.

Toxic emotions are what consume our thoughts and keep us stuck. They can poison our minds, take over our thinking, become an obsession and eventually even make us sick—studies have shown an increase in diseases like cancer when a person has unhealed emotional trauma.

On a practical level, when you're in the grip of toxic emotions, you can't dream big. You inhibit your ability to show up for yourself. You aren't able to adopt peak-performance habits such as discipline, which are necessary for you to take action towards your goals and dreams.

If you don't want negative emotions to become toxic, you need to expose them to the light, and actively deal with them in a healthy, constructive manner. It's not easy to start, but it makes so much sense once you've got the hang of it.

But before that, how do you replace existing toxic emotions with new, positive ones? In this case, you have to rewrite your narrative, changing your emotional perspective and attachment to the event that caused the emotions in the first place. Yes, easier said than done!

If parts of this book are feeling uncomfortable to you, or if you are feeling resistance towards a particular methodology, topic or exercise, you're going to need to push through and challenge yourself to embrace a new way of thinking.

Acknowledge that it is your thinking that is responsible for the state you currently find yourself in—and old ways of thinking will not bring about new behaviours or change.

"The truth is, unless you let go, unless you forgive yourself, unless you forgive the situation, unless you realise the situation is over, you cannot move forward."

– Steve Maraboli

Remember that your brain's primary function is to keep you safe and comfortable.

Your brain seeks the familiar, especially when it comes to feelings. Believe it or not, if you've been miserable or depressed for most of your life, then your brain wants to keep you in that state because there is comfort in the familiar.

If feeling joyful or happy is strange to you, you'll have to fight your own thoughts in order to break free from your addiction to your familiar depressed state. It takes tremendous courage, awareness and effort to break free and break through.

Letting go of your past narrative and old ways of thinking is like ripping off a Band-Aid. You experience mental pain because:

1. You're clinging to memories from the past.
2. You've become addicted to past feelings.
3. There's a perceived benefit in holding on to an emotion that's become toxic.

It's irritating when someone says, "Just let it go." It's not like we can shake our hands and all our undesirable emotions, thoughts and feelings just fall to the ground. The process of letting go is about replacing one pattern of thinking and feeling with a new pattern. Growth isn't only about learning something new; before that, the old has to die.

You cannot create a new way of living if your mind is full of old ideas—just like you cannot hold something if your hands are already full.

Breaking up with a person is never a pleasant experience—there's always a certain amount of pain involved. I'm asking you to break up with an idea, thought, emotion or feeling that you've held close for many years, maybe even your whole life. The pain may be similar to a romantic breakup.

You may ask, "What am I without this memory?" But if what you're holding on to keeps you in a state of mental suffering, I can guarantee that the answer is, "A more whole and happy you." The key is to train yourself to be stronger than your thoughts.

The reward of this work is a shift from a fear-based response to a response rooted in love.

You are not your thoughts: you are the observer behind your thinking. You have the power to accept or reject any thought that comes into your mind, and you have 100% control in deciding which thoughts to act on. If you truly want a breakthrough or multiple breakthroughs (yes, even men can have those!), then you need to acquire new ways of thinking. You need to start showing up for yourself, as the objective observer, showing your thoughts that you are the boss.

If you want to choose a new state of mind—happiness, joy, excitement, empowerment, peace—then your thoughts need to adapt to allow in the new feeling.

It sounds very simple—and it really is.

Chapter 15
Four Toxic Emotions:
Anger, Resentment, Guilt and Shame

It's important to realise that with any toxic emotion there's a perceived benefit, which is often why we find it hard to let go. For example, being angry evokes a strong emotion—it makes us feel alive and gives us an instant rush of energy. Anger can be directed into a heavy gym workout or a cause we feel passionate about. If it's that useful, why would we let go of anger?

Let's explore these emotions in more depth.

Anger and Resentment

Anger and resentment are emotions that are directed outwards, towards someone or something outside of you. You hold the belief that someone shouldn't have treated you in a particular way, or that something shouldn't have happened the way it did. This is resistance; you are fighting against life.

Because it requires an external trigger, anger is often understood as a secondary emotion. The primary emotion of anger is always pain—in other words, pain triggers anger. You may prefer to be angry than to sit with the pain because anger is a great way to escape from feelings of vulnerability. Anger creates a false sense of power, even control. Anger also creates an explosive emotional charge that heightens your senses—so being angry can make us feel alive. But the things we do and say while angry can result in more problems, creating a negative cycle over and above the pain we've tried to avoid by being angry in the first place.

Maybe a romantic partner or family member says something nasty to you. It hurts. As you react in anger, you say something even more hurtful or retaliate with physical aggression. This creates more issues, more drama, instead of a peaceful conclusion.

Or maybe you're still angry because of something someone did to you years ago—maybe it was a bad joke, or they did something without thinking. You didn't have the courage to confront them or deal with the situation at the time, which left a feeling of resentment. The other person has no idea how you're feeling—for them, everything is hunky-dory, but every time you see them, your simmering anger disrupts your own mental space.

Anger and resentment are always linked to blame: you feel that others are responsible for making you angry. The emotion of anger can be compared to you drinking poison and expecting the other person to die: the person involved might have forgotten about the issue, but when you hold on to anger and resentment, they become toxic. And because they are based on the actions of others, they keep you in a state of reactivity and victimisation.

Guilt and Shame

Whereas anger and resentment are directed at someone else or a situation outside of you, guilt and shame are directed inwards, towards yourself.

Guilt is linked to something you have done: you feel guilt when you believe you have done something wrong. It often points to something that isn't aligned with your values or beliefs. Maybe you stole something, spoke badly of someone, broke a promise, betrayed someone's trust, caused hurt or pain. Guilt is always linked to a tangible act that can be clearly identified.

While guilt is linked to an event or act, shame is anchored to your identity. Guilt says, "I did something bad." Shame says, "I am bad." Shame is a general feeling of judging and negatively valuing yourself. Feelings of guilt can often lead to shame—your individual actions compound to build up the negative picture you hold of yourself, triggering the belief that you're a bad person, and leading you to feel that you are less than, not enough, undeserving or even worthless.

Having low self-worth leads to low self-love and self-compassion, and a lack of self-respect—you may have a tendency to beat yourself up or to punish yourself. When you don't value yourself, you're more likely to get into a self-destructive cycle of excessive drinking, drug use or other irresponsible behaviours.

My own destructive pattern of guilt and shame

For me, guilt and shame were my greatest stumbling blocks.

Right from when I first started drinking as a teenager, I was abusive under the influence of alcohol. When I was drunk or high, I became a monster, emotionally abusing the people I loved the most. I would lash out, using a person's greatest insecurities against them, trying to make them feel useless. When I woke up the next morning, the previous night would be a blur and I'd feel horrendous about the things I'd said and done. And I knew no apology or showering of "guilt gifts" could undo my actions.

In time, I came to despise the man I was, and because I held on to that guilt and shame and never confronted it head-on, I felt undeserving of love and success. Captive to the image of myself as unworthy, unlovable, bad, despicable and disgusting, I blocked any potential breakthroughs—and as soon as I started to see progress in my life, I'd self-sabotage. I kept myself stuck, repeatedly taking refuge in alcohol and drugs.

Guilt and shame drove my self-talk. I constantly reminded myself how useless and worthless I was, and my self-destructive cycle continued throughout my twenties. I'd build up a business, and then go on a bender and destroy it. If I felt my partner truly loved me, I'd destroy the relationship. Success and love were just not congruent with the belief I held that I was utterly unworthy and undeserving.

I can tell you with absolute certainty that if you do not deal with your guilt and shame, it will grow into an Everest-sized mountain. The longer you wallow in these feelings, the worse they get.

Guilt and shame will keep you stuck. Trust me, I have plenty of experience.

Turn that frown upside down

Remember when I said there are no bad emotions? Well, after hearing my story you may be questioning my sanity here…

The thing is, emotions like anger, resentment, guilt and shame become toxic when you hold on to them. But in small doses, the discomfort of these emotions can push you into taking the action you need in your life—and in this way, they can be our greatest help.

For example, when you encounter a problem you feel strongly about, anger can motivate you to find solutions, set boundaries or join a cause. As an emotion that builds up over time, resentment may increase your pain until you are prompted to address the source. Guilt can point to an area where you know you've done wrong—the healthy response is to apologise for affecting someone else in a negative way, and to make it right. Shame is rooted in self-judgment. Feeling shame gives you an opportunity to correct yourself and change your patterns of behaviour.

To move forward in crafting a *vision* for your life and taking massive *action* towards it, you need to choose to:

- Shift from anger and resentment to love, kindness and empathy;
- Shift from guilt and shame to self-love, self-worth and value.

The key is to take *ownership* and make the change.

TAKE ACTION!

- Are you holding on to anger, resentment, guilt or shame? What are the events or reasons behind these feelings?
- What impact will holding on to these feelings have in three months, one year, five years?
- How much pain are you causing yourself?

Chapter 16
Tools to Reframe Anger and Resentment

In order to replace your toxic emotions, you need to change what an event means to you by reframing the story and rewriting your perspective—because if you change the meaning, you shift the emotion. Teachers like Joe Dispenza and Tony Robbins explain that where focus goes, energy flows. You can choose to focus on the pain, or you can shift your focus to the lesson in the painful experience.

TAKE ACTION!

To reframe your relationship with anger and resentment, think of a triggering event and ask yourself:

- How did the situation serve you?
- What did you learn?
- How did you grow?
- How did the situation impact others in a way that inspired connection and growth?

When you realise that you've grown because of what's happened to you, and that everything is the perfect experience you needed to have, then you can let go of toxic emotions and replace them with gratitude.

If you can't find any growth narratives attached to an event or anything to be grateful for, then here are three tools you can use.

TOOL #1: THE VILLAIN'S BACK STORY

Every villain has a back story. The more evil the "villain" in your life, the more horrific their upbringing and the pain and suffering they've probably endured.

I don't believe that people are inherently bad or evil. When someone does you wrong, they are usually acting out their own past hurts—patterns that they themselves have not dealt with. The truth is that hurt people hurt people. Everyone is doing the best they can with the tools they have.

Think of someone you are angry at or hold resentment towards. Now imagine their back story. Imagine what they have possibly gone through—what has enabled them to inflict pain? What deep hurt and trauma could they be dealing with? What are their demons?

I've found this to be a particularly effective tool. Here's an example of how it went down. One of my friends was holding a lot of anger towards a woman who was bullying her at work. She told me, "Devon, I hate her," and went on to explain how this woman made constant digs at her.

I asked my friend to close her eyes and imagine what may have led this person to behave like this. I painted a vivid picture: "What if both her parents died young, leaving her an orphan? She was then adopted by a foster family, who verbally, physically and sexually abused her. Imagine that she later faced severe abuse in all of her relationships because her abandonment wounds from childhood only attracted narcissistic men into her life. What if all she has ever known is pain and suffering? Now imagine that when she bullies you, it's a subconscious, automatic response to trauma that has kept her safe from even more feelings of hurt and despair."

I asked my friend, "Holding on to this projection, how do you feel about her now?"

My friend sighed. "Wow," she said, with tears in her eyes. "I feel really sorry for her."

What my friend proved is how quickly a feeling of anger can be exchanged for compassion and empathy—emotions that are rooted in love. Remember, this was my friend's anger we were dealing with, not the bully's. The real facts of the bully's life didn't actually matter—what mattered was the narrative my friend was telling herself. By releasing herself from the feeling of being bullied, she stopped feeling like a victim and empowered herself to actually address the situation.

> "The practice of forgiveness is our most important contribution to the healing of the world."
>
> – Marianne Williamson

If you have the capacity to shift the narrative and rewrite the story, you're also able to switch from anger to love—and that is 100% up to you. The only reason you would hold on to the anger is because you choose to, which also means that you are responsible for when your suffering will end. The choice is yours.

TOOL #2: FORGIVE AND FORGET

Another tool that has helped me has been to write a letter to the person I'm angry with, saying that I forgive them, and giving the reasons why I forgive them.

This is a symbolic act you can take in order to let go. You don't need to give the letter to the person—you can just write it, read it aloud to yourself and then throw it away—or even burn it, if that's best for you. Forgiveness will set you free.

TOOL #3: WISH THEM WELL

For 21 days, wish the person who hurt you well. You may think this is crazy, but it's about creating a repetitive act that will slowly change your state of being. In your daily prayer, meditation, journalling or however you process your thoughts, send the person a blessing. In time, you too will be blessed, because you will be free of anger and resentment.

Remember, all of this is not about the other person or the situation: this is about you shifting the emotions that are keeping you stuck. Letting go of anger and resentment is part of taking *ownership* and being accountable for your own growth.

If you want to break free, you need to shift from fear towards love.

Chapter 17
Tools to Reframe Guilt and Shame

Guilt and shame can feel completely overwhelming. Having low self-esteem and a destructive inner voice can overshadow any positive image you might have of yourself. Minimising your guilt and shame is essential to you breaking free and moving forward: once you've made your story of guilt and shame smaller than you thought it was, you can go to work on reprogramming your narrative.

The thing with shame is that it exists in secrecy. Shame whispers to you in the dark: You are not enough, you're undeserving, you're a bad person. But this voice loses its power when you verbalise the experience yourself. Having the courage to bring your shame to light will free you.

TAKE ACTION!

To reframe your relationship with shame and guilt, think of a triggering event and ask yourself:

- How did the situation serve you?
- What did you learn?
- How did you grow?
- How can you use this experience to be there for someone else?

At rehab, one of my greatest breakthroughs was sharing my most shameful experiences with my counsellor. Before that, I'd thought I was the only person who'd endured such shocking situations—only to hear that my counsellor had had many similar experiences, some even worse than mine. When he shared his stories with me, I felt a weight lifting off my shoulders—I wasn't the only one, and I wasn't alone. That is the power of shared human experience.

TOOL #1: SHARE YOUR STORY

Part of the magic of Narcotics Anonymous and Alcoholics Anonymous is that they provide a safe space in which to share your story with complete strangers. The one thing that connects every person in a meeting is the dysfunctional thinking that has driven their behaviours and actions.

Find safe spaces in which to reach out and share your story in a spirit of mutual support. This can be to a friend or family member, or through more formal structures like those I used.

When we listen to other people's stories, we feel connected to something far greater than our own struggle. Knowing that you're not alone helps you to minimise your guilt and shame. When you release yourself from guilt and shame, you give others permission to do the same—a victory for you is a victory for all.

If I hadn't gone through my alcoholism and addiction, I wouldn't be able to relate to the people who are stuck where I used to be, and I wouldn't have the tools or the ability to help anyone achieve their own breakthrough. The most painful moments of my life have become the backbone of my most empowering narrative, one I use to try to touch people's lives and make a difference. Pain has transformed into purpose. My mess has become my message. Yours can too.

TOOL #2: FORGIVE YOURSELF

To let go of guilt and shame, you need to forgive yourself. This is often harder than forgiving someone else, but it is such a vital step.

You can do this by looking in the mirror and forgiving yourself out loud. If this is too uncomfortable for you, write yourself a letter. Once you are done, read it out loud. You can read it as many times as you like, whenever you feel guilt and shame surfacing along your journey. If you don't want to keep the letter, read it once, then burn it.

Set yourself free, stop the self-punishment and allow yourself to step into your purpose.

Growth is not just about what you can learn and pick up, it's also about what you can put down and replace. It's about letting go of your baggage and replacing disempowering thoughts, feelings, emotional states and behaviours with empowering ones.

The journey of letting go of guilt and shame is about replacing them with self-love and self-worth—and it's a journey well worth taking.

Chapter 18
Your Hero Story

―――――――

*Hard times don't create heroes. It is during the hard times when the "hero"
within us is revealed.*
– Bob Riley

―――――――

Phew—that's been tough!

It's never easy to look at the darker aspects of ourselves, so if you've made it through the last few chapters, well done! There's good stuff ahead. Taking radical ownership of your past and present is about essentially shifting from victim to victor by rewriting your narrative so that you become the hero.

Victims have a tendency to blame. Victims resist reality and use it as an excuse to stay stuck. Victims are constantly in denial; they lack the belief that they are responsible for their own thoughts, emotions and actions. Victims ask, "Why me?" "Why is life so unfair?" Victims live in this disempowered state.

Victors take ownership. Victors assume full accountability for their thoughts, feelings and actions, past and present. Victors take responsibility and know that they have the power to decide on their state of being. Victors ask "How?" questions: "How did that serve me?" "How can I learn and grow from this?" "How can I use this for my good and the good of others?"

No-one can choose for you whether you become a victim or a victor: the choice is yours alone. What I can say is that those who play the victim in their own story aren't empowered to create a vision that gets them excited, and they certainly don't have the energy or discipline to take action towards their goals and dreams.

This is where it starts: taking **ownership** of your story—past, present and future.

Ultimately, everything you've been through has equipped you for your greatest purpose of all: to serve others.

"...turn a mess into a message, a test into a testimony, a trial into triumph, a victim into a victor."

– Fern Bernstein

SUMMARY OF OWNERSHIP

- In this section on *ownership*, we have discussed a number of important ideas that will lay the foundation for growth in your life.
- The place where you get most stuck is in your own thinking. To shift from suffering to growth, you need to master your mindset.
- Mastery starts with becoming aware of what is keeping you stuck.
- You have no control over the events or circumstances that happen outside of you.
- But you have total control over your *perception* of these events.
- When you rewrite your narrative, you change the thoughts attached to events.
- You are able to decide whether your thoughts will fuel an empowered or a disempowered narrative.
- Your thoughts determine your feelings, and your thoughts and feelings work together to drive your actions.
- Every experience is the perfect experience for you to grow. Resistance to our experiences is often at the root of our suffering.
- The greatest growth happens in dark places.
- Pain is inevitable, but there is always purpose in pain. Pain, obstacles and challenges are there to push you to take *action* and grow.
- You suffer when you anchor your identity to the pain and resist the lesson.
- Surrender and acceptance, as a way of life, will relieve you from anxiety, stress and suffering.
- Taking radical *ownership* means knowing that you are 100% responsible for bringing about the changes you want to experience.
- When you hold on to them, anger, resentment, guilt and shame have the potential to become toxic.
- Letting go of toxic emotions is vital for you to get unstuck.
- You have the power to shift from victim to victor, and be the hero of your own story.
- Your greatest purpose is to serve those who are suffering the way you have suffered.

Part 2
Vision

Man, alone, has the power to transform his thoughts into physical reality; man, alone, can dream and make his dreams come true.
– Napoleon Hill

In our three-step process, we need to first take ownership before crafting a vision and putting it into action. When we don't fully take ownership, we hold on to the emotions that keep us stuck, which limits our ability to tap into our potential. Holding toxic emotions exhausts us, leaving us feeling hopeless and disempowered. Then the next two steps feel like a mammoth task—like carrying that 100kg backpack or running down the street with an open parachute.

That's why we have to get rid of anything that weighs us down: we have to let go, so we can travel light and free. So whatever you do, don't skip the first step—because when we hold on to beliefs that are rooted in fear, we can't dream big, and our vision is a watered-down version of our truth.

If you haven't done the exercises, I encourage you to go back through Part 1 and get stuck in. If you've done the work, awesome! Let's move on to crafting your vision.

In Part 2, we answer these questions:

- Why is it so important to have a vision?
- What stands in the way of you creating your vision?
- How do you create a vision for every area of your life?
- Once you have your vision, how do you set goals and milestones to get there?

To craft our vision, we'll be looking at some of the best tools available from teachers working in the field of personal transformation.

So, having taken complete *ownership* of your past and where you are in the present moment, you can now look forward to the future. It's time to let your imagination run wild, to create in your mind the life of your dreams.

Chapter 19
The Importance of Having a Vision

The only thing worse than being blind is having sight but no vision.
– Helen Keller

Having a *vision* is vitally important. Without one, you're like a boat bobbing about on the ocean without sails or a rudder, at the mercy of the winds and the waves. This feeling of drifting aimlessly through life without direction creates immense anxiety and frustration.

So how do you break free from a perpetual holding pattern?

How do you chart a course of direction?

You might be too young to remember, but there was a time when a road trip was incomplete without a large map that folded out awkwardly across the entire dashboard. Thank goodness for technological advances—every phone now has a range of map and GPS apps to get you from A to B. The thing about a GPS, though, is that it's useless if you don't know your destination.

You need to know where you want to go.

Maybe you wake up every morning, get out on the same side of the bed, brush your teeth, dress the same way you always do, take the same route to work, go to the shops, train at the gym and then come home. If you repeat this cycle day in and day out, week after week, month after month, without having a clear vision for your life, then you're going to go as far as that rudderless boat bobbing in the ocean.

The thing is, we humans have a need to evolve, to feel a sense of progress and accomplishment—and when we don't know what we want in life, we experience stress and frustration. Not wanting to face uncomfortable feelings, we become masters of procrastination as we look for an escape, a way to drown them out. You might escape this repetitive cycle of boredom through drinking, drugs, sex, unhealthy relationships, gambling, gaming, eating too much or many other kinds of time-consuming obsessions—behaviours that steal the precious, valuable time that could be used to move you towards your dream life. That's why it's so important to craft a vision for yourself. If we don't have a vision for our future, we're going to endlessly repeat our patterns from the past.

So, where do we begin?

There are three components that work together like a satellite guidance system: vision, mission and purpose.

Your vision is the overall picture of what your future looks like and where you aspire to be. It's what you see when you arrive at your destination—an inspiring picture of your future that excites you to the core.

Your mission is about how you actually show up each day to create that vision. From the time you wake up in the morning, your mission paints a picture of how you are taking action and who you are serving.

Your purpose is the reason you are on this earth—it's why you exist. Your purpose is fundamentally linked to your deepest values and what is most important to you.

They can be summarised like this:

- Vision asks, "Where am I going?" It's the force that inspires you.
- Mission asks, "What am I doing?" It's the force that drives you.
- Purpose asks, "Why am I doing it?" It's the force that guides you.

In the OVA method, we focus on vision because it describes in detail what your world looks like if your mission is successful and you have followed your purpose. While it's important that you have absolute clarity, your vision is not set in stone. Where you want to be may change in a few weeks', months' or years' time. Your vision will evolve as you do, and you can change it as your journey unfolds.

But as a starting point, right now, in whatever season of life you may find yourself, it's time to think about what you want. Because knowing what you want forms the foundation of your dream life.

Chapter 20
What Do You Want?

The first secret of getting what you want is knowing what you want.
— Arthur D Hlavaty

The same way you have to plug your destination into your GPS, the first question you need to ask yourself when creating your vision is, "What do I want?"

Many people know with great clarity what they don't want in life. They know what they don't want in their career, from their romantic partner or from life in general. And often, that's why they attract more of exactly that—because when you focus on what you don't want, you tend to attract even more of it.

> "What you think you become. What you feel you attract. What you imagine you create."
> — Buddha

The Law of Attraction is a universal law that has had a powerful effect in many areas of my life. If you'd like to dive a bit deeper, I would highly recommend that you read *The Secret* by Rhonda Byrne (you've probably heard of it already—it's not that much of a secret anymore!), and *Ask and It Is Given* by Esther and Jerry Hicks. These will give you a deep understanding of how this law can be used in your life. Basically, the Law of Attraction explains how the focus of our attention attracts certain things into our lives. To put it another way, it uses the power of the mind to translate our thoughts into material reality.

Just think about that for a moment.

If you focus on doom and gloom, you will remain under that cloud. If you focus on positive goals, you will find a way to achieve them. It all starts on the screen of your mind.

"You create your thoughts, your thoughts create your intentions and your intentions create your reality."
– Wayne Dyer

For many years, I've followed philosopher and author Bob Proctor's work through his online conferences and courses. He makes the point that every material man-made thing—every invention and anything you can see right now as you look around you—first started as a thought in someone's mind. With clear intentions, those thoughts translated into the pen on your desk, the light bulb in your lamp, a rocket ship that can fly to space…

The more I make use of the Law of Attraction, the more magical occurrences happen in my life, and with increasing frequency.

Let me share a few examples with you.

One morning I was thinking of an old friend of mine, Brendan, who had moved to Los Angeles. I was curious to know how life in LA was going, but we hadn't spoken in

"Thoughts become things. If you see it in your mind, you will hold it in your hand."
– Bob Proctor

more than six years. I didn't have any contact details for him and he wasn't on social media. I thought to myself that I needed to find a way to get hold of him, and then I went about my day and forgot all about it. Later that afternoon I received a call on my phone from an unknown number. I answered, and to my complete shock it was Brendan! He said he was visiting family in South Africa for two weeks, and would love to catch up.

Coincidence or God-incidence?

The Law of Attraction works on all levels, big and small, from the sublime to the ridiculous. I ran out of hair gel one morning, just as I was getting ready for an important meeting. Instead of getting frustrated, I thought to myself, "The universe has my back and it'll take care of me." The meeting was due to start in half an hour, but somehow I knew I'd be ready. Driving to the office, I pulled up to a traffic light and, lo and behold, a group of promoters were handing out sample tubs of the exact brand of hair gel I use. No way, right?

I'm now no longer surprised when a thought in my mind turns to reality in next to no time. I imagine standing on a stage speaking to an audience, and the next day I get invited to speak at a conference for 100 people. I imagine meeting an amazing woman, and the same afternoon I bump into someone at the gym, and we immediately hit it off. I imagine writing my first book and now here you are reading it.

Remember that you give life to every thought you have.

But there's an important proviso. Just as in the experiment where you are told, "Do not picture a pink elephant," and that's all you can see, the creative force that makes your thoughts real in the physical world does not work in the negative.

So when you say, "I do not want drama in my life," it only hears "drama in my life." This is why, right now, you have to be ultra-specific on what you do want in your life, and you need to stop focusing on what you don't want.

Deal?

TAKE ACTION!
- What do you want in life? Write a list of whatever pops into your mind. Don't censor or edit yourself. Just allow the ideas to *flow*.

Chapter 21
Who Do You Want to Be?

You're under no obligation to be the same person you were five minutes ago.
– Alan Watts

When it comes to crafting a vision, we often think about the things we want in life: big house, cars, island holidays, multiple businesses, the money to make it all happen… You need to dig deeper. You need to think about who you want to become as a person.

Who do you want to be?

There is a compelling video of Matthew McConaughey accepting the 2014 Oscar for Best Actor for his role in *Dallas Buyers Club*. In his speech, he shared this powerful story.

When I was 15 years old, I had a very important person in my life come to me and say, "Who's your hero?"

And I said, "I don't know. I gotta think about that. Give me a couple of weeks."

I come back two weeks later. This person comes up and says, "Who's your hero?"

I said, "I thought about it. You know who it is? It's me in 10 years."

So I turned twenty-five 10 years later, and that same person comes to me and says, "So, are you a hero?"

And I was like, "Not even close. No, no, no." She said, "Why?"

I said, "Because my hero's me at 35."

So you see, every day, every week, every month and every year of my life, my hero's always 10 years away. I'm never gonna be my hero. I'm not gonna attain that. I know I'm not, and that's just fine with me because that keeps me with somebody to keep on chasing.

So, who do you want to be?

What characteristics and qualities do you show up with? Do you want to be kind, giving, loving, wise, strong? Do you want to be a person who other people can trust, someone who's approached for advice, who invests in others, who shares wisdom? How do you have an impact on the world, and what difference do you make? What do people say about you?

When you can visualise who you want to become, you have someone you can keep on chasing.

TAKE ACTION!
- Write down a number of different admirable qualities that you aspire to represent, and spend some time reflecting on them.
- Describe yourself 10 years from now. What will people say about you? How will this make you feel?

When you know with absolute clarity what type of person you want to be, you can choose to adopt those characteristics right this second. When you have a clear picture of who that future person is, and you know why you want to be that person, you will be able to hold yourself accountable for stepping into that version of yourself.

Tom and Lisa Bilyeu are co-founders of Impact Theory, a media platform they launched in 2016 to share knowledge and leave a positive mark on the world. Impact Theory is one of my favourite YouTube channels—I find the interviews wise and insightful. Tom's personal story is remarkable. He went from being depressed and sleeping on his sister's couch to co-founding Quest Nutrition, now famous for its protein bars, which was transformed from an idea to a company valued at over $1-billion in just five years. Today, Tom's personal net worth totals over $400-million.

In a video of a keynote address, Tom says that humans are the ultimate adaptation machine.

Just by being human, each and every one of you is capable of great change. Who you are today does not predict who you can become. Who you can become is the answer to a very simple question: what do you want and what price are you willing to pay to get there?

> "A vision is not just a picture of what could be; it is an appeal to our better selves, a call to become something more."
>
> – Rosabeth Moss Kanter

The price you have to pay is doing the work. It involves making the effort to craft your vision and then to take action. The price you have to pay is letting go of the old version of yourself, knowing that there is so much more for you to step into.

For me, creating a vision for myself was incredibly difficult. My self-image used to be that of a man who was manipulative, divisive, dishonest, abusive and unkind. The image I held of myself was marred by my deep attachment to anger, resentment, guilt, shame and self-hatred. I had to deconstruct this vile portrait by rewriting my narrative, and the perception and meaning I'd anchored to past events.

It was only after I had put to bed the old version of myself that I could begin to dream of who I wanted to be. This process started during my rehab, but it has never stopped. I often ask myself the question: Who do I want to be?

When I first started thinking of who I wanted to be, my main motivation was to right the wrongs of my past and make amends. I felt I had a duty to balance out my karmic energy by making up for a lot of the bad I had done.

I crafted a vision of myself as a kind man who is loving, giving and focused on serving others. Because of my destructive past behaviour, I envisaged a man who now built people up, who inspired growth and contributed more than he took from life. But it was tough going.

The vision I created felt a long way away from the person who, just four months before, had walked up the steps of the rehabilitation centre. But I knew my vision was the true me, buried deep inside my soul, eager to come out.

Today I've made this process part of my daily spiritual practice. In my morning reflection, I close my eyes and picture not just the man I want to become, but also the man I want to show up as on that day. Having clarity about this always brings a smile to my face and I go about my day acting as though I already am that man. It's empowering and inspiring, and gives me insane amounts of energy, especially when I'm facing obstacles, challenges or painful situations.

In the moment, I can rise above and choose to step up as the man I'm destined to become.

TAKE ACTION!

- When you meditate or have quiet time in the morning, close your eyes and imagine the person you want to be. Think about the characteristics and qualities of that person. In your mind, play through the day that lies ahead of you, and see how the best version of you will tackle the tasks at hand. What is your state? How do you feel? How do you make others feel?

Chapter 22
Clarity Is Power

Clarity of vision is the key to achieving your objectives.
– Tom Steyer

I've always been a dreamer, and the older I get, the clearer my dreams are becoming. These days, when I close my eyes and imagine my life 10 years from now, I can see exactly where I am, who I've become, who I'm surrounded by, what I'm doing and why I'm doing it.

But back when I was caught up in the swirl of alcoholism and addiction, I was so consumed with getting by that I had no capacity to dream. I was consumed by my stuff, trying desperately to run away from the pain I'd been avoiding since childhood. I had no clarity on the direction I was heading in, and I found myself drifting endlessly in circles, immensely frustrated that there was no forward action.

After every relapse, when I'd disappear from work and miss important deadlines, I had so much mess to clean up that I didn't have time to set clear intentions for where I wanted to be. Life was a blur.

In the absence of clearly defined goals, we become strangely loyal to performing daily trivia, until we ultimately become enslaved by it... On the flip side, in the presence of clearly defined and embodied goals, we become strangely loyal to the achievement of every single one automatically.

– Peggy McColl

The destructive patterns that had taken up permanent residence in my mind had to be removed to open up space where something new could be created. It was only in rehab, when I started to heal and face my traumas head-on, that I could begin to create the mental space and capacity to start imagining a new life for myself.

In my years of sobriety, my vision has become so razor-sharp that I can see my future with absolute clarity, and I'm now amazed how quickly I can attract good breaks, people and opportunities into my life.

TAKE ACTION!

The clearer you get about your goals and what you want to achieve, the easier it is to make progress towards them. You need to know exactly what you want in every area of your life, so think about these questions and write down the answers:

- What things do you want to have?
- What kind of person do you want to become?
- What do you want to experience?
- What adventures would you like to go on?
- How will you leave a positive legacy?
- What impact can you have on future generations?

When a clear picture emerges in your mind, it becomes easy to create an action plan with tangible milestones and goals. An uncertain, wishy-washy vision won't inspire you. The clearer you can be about what you want, the easier it will be to plot the right path on your exciting journey.

Chapter 23
Creating Balance

By now you should understand the importance of clarity and detail—but maybe you're still not clear on what areas of your life you need to think about in creating your vision. Or perhaps you're crystal-clear on certain goals, like those related to health and fitness, but a bit clueless about how to fit family and friends into the mix, and you're wondering how that affects your vision of the future.

Balance is vital for you to be a well-rounded and whole human being. It doesn't help if you're thriving in your career but your home life's a disaster—the key to fulfilment is to balance your awareness, focus and attention across all areas of your life.

The Wheel of Life is a popular coaching tool used to visually represent how balanced you are across all areas of your life. It helps us see where we may be out of balance, and what areas of our lives might need a bit more attention (and intention!).

The Wheel of Life

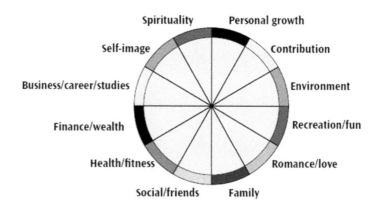

TAKE ACTION!

Copy this Wheel of Life, or print one out from the internet. Use it to think about your life in terms of these areas:

- Personal growth
- Contribution/charity/volunteering
- Environment
- Recreation/fun
- Romance/love
- Family
- Social/friends
- Health/fitness
- Finance/wealth
- Business/career/studies
- Self-image
- Spirituality

Give yourself a rating according to how fulfilled you feel, 10 being highly fulfilled and 1 being unfulfilled.

Draw a line from each point all the way around the circle.

This will give you a sense of your personal balance.

Now write down what you'd like to see, experience and accomplish in each of these areas in the next five to 10 years.

Give particular focus to areas where you gave yourself a lower score. Really push yourself to think more about how you will insert energy into this area.

It's important to note that all areas of your life don't have to be in balance all the time. In different seasons of life, different aspects will be of greater or lesser importance; for example, in your twenties, your career may take greater focus than family needs. But in each season, the more balanced you can be, the more joy and fulfilment you'll experience.

Writing down your vision for each area is like putting a destination into your GPS that will ultimately help you create a better balance—because remember, all work and no play makes inspiration run away.

Chapter 24
Values and Beliefs

It's not hard to make decisions when you know what your values are.
– Roy Disney

Whether you're aware of them or not, your values and beliefs are powerful forces that drive your behaviour. This is what makes every person unique: we adopt values and beliefs throughout our lives, based on our distinct experiences and the meanings or beliefs we attach to them.

Let's get a better understanding of why becoming more aware of your values and beliefs is so important as you start the process of crafting your vision. (And don't worry, we'll be getting there in Chapter 28—there's just a bit of theory to get through first.)

Values

Values are personal principles that you hold in high regard. Your values are what is most important to you—the qualities according to which you live your life. They are your compass, guiding who you become and how you act.

When your values are in sync with how you live your life (what you do and how you behave), you will generally feel good. Living out of sync with your values makes you feel disconnected, like something just doesn't feel right. When you shape your vision around your values, you honour your authenticity, and it's easier to move forward to achieve your goals. This is why it's so important for you to know your core values—the values that are most important to you.

Let's look at an example. You might have the vision of running a large business with staff across the globe, but maybe one of your highest values is spending time with your family. If running your business involves 16-hour workdays and frequent overseas trips, you're not going to be seeing much of your family. And even if your business is a runaway success, you won't find joy in the process of achieving your vision. Do you see what I mean about having your vision and values aligned?

It's also important to remember that your values will shift through the seasons of your life. As mentioned, family time may not be one of your highest values when you're in your twenties, when you're placing more value on financial growth and rising up the corporate ladder. Your values are likely to shift—the trick is to know where you are, and to identify what's most important to you in this season.

You'll know your vision is aligned with your values when you experience feelings of excitement and happiness about achieving your vision. As with everything relating to growth, awareness is key.

TAKE ACTION!

Go through this list of core values[7]:

Achievement	Family	Peace
Adventure	Friendships	Pleasure
Authenticity	Fun	Poise
Authority	Growth	Popularity
Autonomy	Happiness	Recognition
Balance	Honesty	Religion
Beauty	Humour	Reputation
Boldness	Influence	Respect
Compassion	Inner harmony	Responsibility
Challenge	Justice	Security
Citizenship	Kindness	Self-respect
Community	Knowledge	Service
Competency	Leadership	Spirituality
Contribution	Learning	Stability
Creativity	Love	Success
Curiosity	Loyalty	Status
Determination	Meaningful	Trustworthiness
Fairness	work	Wealth
Faith	Openness	Wisdom
Fame	Optimism	

Write down all the values that are important to you.

Now go through the values you've chosen, and select your top five: these are your core values. When you start to write down your goals later in this section, keep in mind these core values. Keep asking yourself, does this *vision* or goal align with my core values? If it does, awesome. If it doesn't, really question whether the goal is authentic to you, or whether it's something you feel obliged to do, perhaps to please someone else.

Beliefs

If your values are the qualities that are most important to you, your beliefs are the ideas, assumptions and convictions that you hold to be true, that feel certain to you. Beliefs are often crafted and formed from our past experiences, from what we have observed or even heard from others, and from societal or religious norms that are passed down to us through our family or community.

The thing with beliefs is that they may not always be true, and often they are a skewed representation of truth. Because our beliefs are the stories we constantly tell ourselves, they have the power to either limit or expand our thinking and our vision.

Your beliefs can be conscious or subconscious. Subconscious beliefs are harder to work on as they lie deep within you, and you often don't notice when and how they affect you. Beliefs can be empowering—they can inspire and push you to take positive action. Or they can be limiting—restricting you and holding you back.

> "The only thing that's keeping you from getting what you want is the story you keep telling yourself."
> – Tony Robbins

Don't limit yourself. Many people limit themselves to what they think they can do. You can go as far as your mind lets you. What you believe, remember, you can achieve.

– Mary Kay Ash

TAKE ACTION!

Here is a list of common limiting beliefs.[8] Read through them a few times to see if any feel familiar to you.

Limiting beliefs about yourself:
- I'm not good enough.
- I'm not pretty/thin enough.
- I'm too old/too young.
- I'm not smart enough.
- I don't have enough time/money.

Limiting beliefs about money:
- I have to work (too) hard to get money.
- Rich people are greedy/evil/unhappy etc.
- My family never had money/being poor runs in our family.
- Money just causes fights about money.
- I'm not good with money.
- I'm always broke/I will never make enough money.

Limiting beliefs about career and business:
- The economy is bad.
- I don't have enough credentials/experience.
- I'm not good at sales/marketing/with numbers etc.

Limiting beliefs about love:
- I don't deserve to be loved.
- I'll never find another partner.
- Love is too painful—I'll get hurt again.
- I'm too stupid/fat/ugly to be loved.

All men are cheats/mean/violent/selfish. All women are clingy/shallow/drama queens/self-involved.

Now let's get real. It seems pretty impossible to create a compelling vision when you feel that you're incapable of achieving the desired outcome. Why would you set yourself an unrealistic task or dream of something that you fundamentally believe you will never achieve?

If that's how you're feeling, then I have great news for you. The beautiful thing about beliefs is that they can be reprogrammed. All it takes is a bit of evidence and a fresh perspective to rewrite a limiting belief into an empowering one.

It's important to recognise that many of the limiting beliefs we hold about ourselves come from childhood trauma. Our core wounds come from events that occurred in childhood, where we might have experienced abandonment, betrayal, rejection, abuse or disapproval. These all lead to the feeling of not being "enough", and this feeds our ultimate fear of not being loved. This is where we pick up a lot of our beliefs about ourselves, especially when it comes to love.

Acknowledging our limiting self-beliefs is important because it's often these beliefs that hold us back from crafting our vision—and then we never really get off the ground.

TAKE ACTION!

If you're interested in exploring more about childhood trauma and core wounds, visit devonbrough.com and have a look at my Relationship Mastery workshop, which I run online, and every month as a face-to-face event.

Setting my vision free: My own story

I know what I'm talking about on this topic, because once again I've been there, done that. Identifying my values and setting myself free from limiting self-beliefs became a huge part of my own transformation.

I started some good personal work in rehab, but since coming out, I've enrolled the services of three coaches—Sam Cowen, Jenna Logan Wait and my best friend, Nikki Loots—to help me shift my mindset from victim-alcoholic-addict mode to the person I am capable of becoming. Given my past, it was the area of my own beliefs where I felt most stuck, where I kept limiting my potential and abilities. I knew I needed to kill off the many limiting beliefs that were keeping me anchored in my past patterns.

With Jenna, I explored how values that didn't align with my vision could become major hurdles. Jenna also helped me identify and replace limiting beliefs with powerful alternatives that would serve a vision for my future—and it was in this area that we got some powerful work done.

In my past, I'd been exposed to many wealthy men who really weren't nice people. Many of them abused alcohol and drugs, and used women purely for sex. After rehab, this was the kind of person I absolutely did not want to be. Although I wanted to grow my personal wealth and create financial abundance, my subconscious belief was that all wealthy men were assholes. I didn't want to be an asshole, so I found that I was sabotaging my own finances through frivolous spending and mismanagement.

Together with Nikki, I used a process called PSYCH-K®[9] to identify the belief, and then reframe it by replacing it with a new belief: "I am a good man. I treat others with love and respect while using my financial abundance to make the world a better place."

Another belief I carried for much of my life was that men caused hurt and were not safe. I'd been abandoned by my father after my parents' separation, bullied by older boys in high school, and taken advantage of by the friend who'd pulled the cheque-book move on me when I was 19 (see Introduction)—so I had a pile of evidence that supported my belief that I wasn't safe around men. I'd always wanted to have good guy friends, mates to hang out with at a braai or sports event, but because of my subconscious belief, I always sabotaged these friendships. It was my internal mechanism for protecting myself from the possibility of getting hurt. Instead, I gravitated towards women and missed out on the camaraderie of male friendship. After I'd identified this belief, I reprogrammed it to: "I am safe opening up to men, and I can experience deep and meaningful relationships with those I meet."

For me, the process of undoing and rewriting subconscious limiting beliefs was immensely rewarding. Sure, it was incredibly frustrating at times as I fought against myself, resisting change, desperately seeking to stay in the comfortable, familiar patterns of thinking. But no pain, no gain—because of course it was in the moments of greatest resistance that I discovered my biggest blocks and identified the areas that needed the most work.

Chapter 25
Smashing Your Limiting Beliefs

You begin to fly when you let go of self-limiting beliefs and allow your mind and aspirations to rise to greater heights.
– Brian Tracy

For years, I held on to the belief that I was not a good writer. My limiting belief held me back from starting a single word or sentence—until I learnt a powerful tool that destroyed it within a single coaching session.

The Tabletop Method

The tabletop method was one of the most useful tools that my performance coach Jenna taught me, and I've used it many times to demolish self-defeating, limiting beliefs that keep me stuck. I still use it today, and will use it for the rest of my life, because as our journey unfolds and we are faced with different challenges, new limiting beliefs will always surface. I come back to this exercise any time I need to replace a limiting belief that is not serving me with one that inspires me to take action.

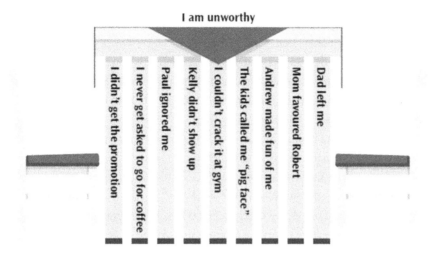

TABLETOP: CORE BELIEF ABOUT YOURSELF

I am unworthy

Dad left me
Mom favoured Robert
Andrew made fun of me
The kids called me "pig face"
I couldn't crack it at gym
Kelly didn't show up
Paul ignored me
I never got asked to go for coffee
I didn't get the promotion

Here's how it works: imagine a simple wooden table. On top of the table is your belief. Each of the legs holding up the table is a story that supports the belief—in other words, a situation or event that provides you with evidence for your belief. These stories you tell yourself hold up your belief and give it support. Your table may have four legs (stories), or you may have six or even more. The longer you've held the belief, the more stories you will have collected to hold it up. The more legs supporting the table, the more powerful the belief.

Now, what happens if you start to break off the table legs? At first, it may not be much—the table may still be quite stable if you only remove one leg. But as you take away another leg, the table will start to wobble. When you've knocked out enough legs, the table will collapse—and with it, the limiting belief on top.

The inverse is true for empowering beliefs. As you add more legs to a table that holds a positive belief, it becomes stronger. To support beliefs that serve you, all you need to do is look for more stories or evidence to support them. With enough legs, your beliefs will be unshakable.

TAKE ACTION!

Let's give the tabletop method a try.

Choose a limiting belief that's holding you back. Really take time to identify where you may be holding limiting beliefs. Where are the blocks in your life? Where do you hold strong beliefs that stand in the way of where you see yourself heading? What is the true cost of holding on to this belief if it keeps you stuck? Once you have it, draw a table on a piece of paper and write this belief on the top.

I'll use the example of the limiting belief that used to hold me back from writing a book. My belief was, "I'm not a good writer."

On the legs of the table, write down all the stories that support this belief. Write down as much evidence as you can think of.

Here are the stories I kept telling myself:

"I've never studied English at university level."

"English was not one of my strong subjects at school—I only got a C."

"My creative director is a brilliant writer; my writing is terrible in comparison."

"I've never practised long-form writing, so I'm probably no good at it."

Choose one of these stories and interrogate its truth. Can you perceive this story in a different way? Can you create a new narrative by choosing a different lens?

In my case: Do you really have to have studied English at university to be a good writer? No.

Now back that up with a fact.

Actually, many authors haven't studied English. My hero, Tony Robbins, didn't even finish high school! (Wow, look at that. I just collapsed that leg!)

Repeat steps 3 and 4 for all the legs holding up your table. When you've collapsed enough legs, you'll discover that the belief is false and the stories you've been telling yourself are not true.

As soon as you've toppled the table, substitute the disempowering or limiting belief with a new empowering belief.

In my case, I swapped out, "I'm not a good writer" for "I'm a great writer."

Find as many stories and pieces of evidence as possible to support this new belief.

I told myself:

"I write catchy social media content and blog posts."

"People always comment on my Instagram posts."

"I'm a great storyteller."

"My words often uplift my friends when they're feeling down."

"People really enjoy my business presentations."

Boom! You've solidified, strengthened and supported a new empowering belief that will push you towards your goals! Repeat this new belief as much as you can, because the old belief may pop back into your mind. With time, though, the new belief will stick and the limiting belief will fall into oblivion.

Embracing Limitless Alternatives

Remember that when it comes to growth, awareness is 90% of the journey, because the first step towards replacing your limiting beliefs with limitless alternatives is to recognise them.

It's also interesting how many limiting beliefs people tend to share. To kick-start your thinking process, read through the following limiting beliefs and their limitless alternatives.[10]

> "I'm not interested in your limiting beliefs; I'm interested in what makes you limitless."
>
> – Brendon Burchard

LIMITING BELIEF	LIMITLESS ALTERNATIVE
About money I'll never have enough money to live the life I want.	There's endless abundance and prosperity for those who work hard and seize it.
It's impossible to become rich unless you come from money.	Anyone can become rich if they have an idea, a plan and determination, and are providing value to others.
About self-worth I'll never be good enough.	I can become my most desired version of myself.
I just wasn't born beautiful, smart, talented, funny etc.	Labels don't define me. I know my worth and the qualities most important to me, regardless of what society thinks is worthy.
About career Everyone hates their job, so why should I expect anything different?	Plenty of people have jobs they love because they take time to get to know themselves and to pursue what makes them happy.

LIMITING BELIEF	LIMITLESS ALTERNATIVE
Only a really qualified person can start their own business, and I'm not one of them.	Anyone can start a business. You don't need a degree or any certifications to come up with a solution that provides value to others.
About relationships I put more effort into my friendships than others do. Either my friends are inconsiderate or I'm just not good enough.	I don't see friendships as a game of quid pro quo. It's my choice to make an effort for those I care about, regardless of how it's reciprocated.
My childhood was painful and difficult. I struggle today because of past trauma in my family.	While I recognise the importance of the events of my past, I don't let them or my relationships define me. I'm not a victim, I'm a victor.
About happiness Most people aren't happy so why should I expect to be?	Other people's inability to be happy has nothing to do with my ability to create happiness for myself.
I'm unhappy because of all of the pain I've experienced throughout my life.	I have the ability to transform any adversity into the seeds of positive change. I recognise that my happiness doesn't depend on the things I experience, but on my attitude towards them.
About change This is just who I am, and I can't change.	I evolve to be better every single day. If I don't like the current version of myself, I can become who I want to be.
I'm overwhelmed. I've always felt this way, and I'll always feel this way.	This too shall pass.

LIMITING BELIEF	LIMITLESS ALTERNATIVE
About success and failure	
If I fail at one thing, then I'm a failure at everything.	I don't let one mistake or failure define me. I see myself as a winner despite experiencing setbacks.
I'd rather not try at all than risk failure.	I'd rather risk failure than never try at all!

So many of the values and beliefs we hold are not even our own—they're passed down to us through the values and beliefs of our parents and mentors, and what we observe in them. Ask yourself whether a particular value or belief is really your own, or whether it's been adopted from someone else. The more you can align your true self, the more authentic you can be and the more joy you will experience in the process.

TAKE ACTION!
- Referring to all the areas of life you are going to work on, write down any limiting beliefs that come to mind.
- Take time and really think of the limiting narratives you have held on to as an excuse not to take action.
- Using the tabletop method, smash these limiting beliefs one by one.

Chapter 26
Authenticity

Authenticity is a collection of choices that we have to make every day. It's about the choice to show up and be real. The choice to be honest. The choice to let our true selves be seen.
– Brené Brown

We're getting closer to crafting our vision, but before we get there we need to talk about authenticity, because it's really important that you are true to your own values and beliefs.

Sometimes, we're shaped and guided by what we think others expect of us. Sometimes, low self-worth means we'd rather people-please than pursue what is of highest importance to us. In order to gain validation from the people, we love, we sometimes create a vision of what our parents, family or romantic partner would expect our lives to look like.

It's so important to have a healthy sense of self-worth, to know that you matter and that your needs and dreams matter.

If you're not clear on your own values and beliefs, you will more easily adopt another person's values and beliefs as your own. The truth is, people-pleasing— saying "yes" when you mean "no"—is a character defect. When you believe that others' needs matter more than your own, you undermine your own self-worth.

Sometimes, parents assert their own unlived dreams onto their children. It may not be coming from a bad place—sometimes our parents think that by coercing us to become a dancer, doctor, engineer or pilot they are setting us up for a life of fulfilment and financial success. But when it comes to your life, you are the captain. You are the only person who should be making choices about what you want to do and where you want to go.

Think of a young person leaving school. They haven't had much time to find themselves or discover a career path they really want to pursue, and perhaps they're under pressure to go study at college or university right away. Let's say their father is an attorney. If they're not sure about what to study, they might follow in their parent's footsteps and enrol to study law. In doing so, they gain approval and affirmation.

They complete their law degree and find themselves in a legal practice. But something just doesn't feel right—they just don't enjoy practising law, and they'd actually be better off working in an artistic field. It might only be years later, during a midlife crisis, that they reassess their life and start to ask what they really want from it.

Actually, it's often in a moment of crisis that we finally take an honest look at ourselves and assess where we stand. But why wait for a crisis? Whatever stage of life you're at, perhaps right now you're feeling stuck because you've pursued someone else's dreams. You may be at the top of your game, but in a career you never wanted. The good news is that it is never too late to pivot. There'll always be a fork in the road, so choose a path that sets your soul on fire. I'm challenging you right now to dig deep and figure out what you want to dedicate your life to.

What inspires you down to your soul? What makes you happy? Your purpose is unique to you; it's something you have to discover for yourself. It's not something that can be handed down through genetics. You have one life—only one! Why dedicate your existence to someone else's dreams?

Authenticity is like a superpower. It creates alignment and helps you tap into a powerful energy that propels you forward. It's incredibly hard to create discipline, to work towards a vision or dream that is not your own. If you are constantly seeking external motivation or inspiration, this could point to the fact that you are not aligned with your true purpose, and that you could be chasing someone else's vision.

The truth is, there are only two people you need to make proud throughout your life: your eight-year-old self and your 80-year-old self. Nothing else matters. When you act with authenticity in your thoughts, words and actions, you don't worry about what anyone else will think. You're honest with yourself, expressing who you truly are. You have no-one else to please.

Self-awareness plays a major role in being authentic. To align with you who truly are, you need to get to know yourself. Spend some time thinking about these questions, and getting clear on the answers:

- What do you desire?
- What do you want?
- Who do you want to become?
- What do you want to do?
- Who do you want to serve?

Authenticity is everything! You have to wake up every day and look in the mirror, and you want to be proud of the person who's looking back at you. And you can only do that if you're being honest with yourself and being a person of high character. You have an opportunity every single day to write that story of your life.

– Aaron Rodgers

When the dream is your own and your vision taps into your purpose, you awaken an unstoppable force. Aligning with your authentic self will have you shooting out of bed in the morning, excited to get to work, taking steps towards achieving your goals and moving towards your vision.

Chapter 27
Feel Your Future Now

The universe doesn't recognise the difference between small goals and big ones; it responds to your emotion and intent.
– Peggy McColl

It's time to let the cat out of the bag. The real reason I want you to get absolutely clear about your vision and to remove any blocks in your way is so that you can experience what your future will feel like right now.

Yes, you read that right. When you create a vision that excites you to the core and you can see your future with absolute clarity, then you can experience what that future feels like immediately. When I do my morning cardio, I walk on the treadmill for 30 minutes and listen to euphoric hard-trance music. (Don't judge me—I like the beats, okay!) As I'm doing that, I walk myself through a typical day in my life five years from now. I see it in my mind with such precision that I begin to experience the feelings that go with it. I often get goosebumps because I can feel the excitement and gratitude welling up inside me.

Your mind is so powerful that you too can project an image onto the fertile screen of your imagination, and your body won't be able to tell whether the feeling is real or just a thought.

This is such a powerful tool to use daily because experiencing desirable feelings in the present moment creates a vibrational field that literally attracts your future towards you—this is the Law of Attraction that we've mentioned before. And don't just take my word for it. I highly recommend checking out Dr Joe Dispenza's work on this topic; he provides meditations that help you create your own visions for the future. (You'll find more details at the back of this book.)

I've used Dr Joe's meditations for more than two years, and I've found them invaluable for feeling into my future and inducing a state of gratitude, joy and excitement. After his meditations, I feel unstoppable, and there's very little that can happen during the day to break my state of **flow**.

TAKE ACTION!

Take a moment to think about your future self. Where will you be? What will you be doing? Who will you be with?

In your mind, take yourself to that future place. Now close your eyes and ask yourself: How do I feel? Are you excited, joyous, grateful, at peace, in love, aligned, serene, courageous, faith-filled, ecstatic, courageous, triumphant?

As you hold on to the vision of your future self, focus all your attention on these feelings. What do you see, smell and hear?

Awaken your senses, and put yourself into that future moment.

How it works is this: a thought enters your subconscious mind and becomes an idea. In your conscious mind, that idea triggers an emotion. The emotion alters your vibration and in turn the energetic field that radiates from you. That vibration or energy is expressed by the actions you take. Your action causes a reaction as the universal field responds to your output. Your actions combined with the reaction create your results. Your results will ultimately dictate the environment, circumstances and conditions in which you find yourself.[11]

The upshot is that when you feed your subconscious a clear thought or image about your future, it will come up with ways to manifest that state. It will create thoughts and ideas that will generate emotions that will inspire actions that will create the results you saw in your mind. In this never-ending loop—and for as long as you hold a clear vision of where you want to be in your mind—ideas will come to you like magic, and you will be a magnet for your vision.

Chapter 28
The Power Life Script™

––––––––––

You define your own life. Don't let other people write your script.
– Oprah Winfrey

––––––––––

In early 2020, when South Africa went into a full national lockdown due to the Covid-19 pandemic, I decided to use the time constructively to focus on my personal growth.

In particular, I wanted to get clearer on my vision. Hunting far and wide for tools that would keep me inspired and motivated, I came across a YouTube video by Peggy McColl, and through it I discovered her Power Life Script™ ebook.[12] I spent a week immersed in what today is one of the most valuable tools I use to stay on track, especially when life's challenges jump out in front of me.

The work begins with you writing the script of your life—and I've come to be such a believer in this process that I'm going to tell you exactly what I did.

I started by writing out a comprehensive story in a Google document, walking through a day in my life in five to 10 years' time. I wrote this in present tense, as if I was actually already there. I kept my descriptions upbeat, focusing on what I want life to be like, and described what I saw and experienced in such vivid detail that I could feel the emotions as though they were real, so that it felt like I was living that life in the present moment. That process took up eight pages, which I then condensed into a four-page version. I then trimmed and refined it even further, to the point where reading it gave me goosebumps almost every time.

I took my script and read it into my MacBook Pro using an external microphone. I pulled this audio file into Adobe's Premiere Pro editing programme, and I added some relaxing meditation music as a background. The final product was a 15-minute audio file that I listen to twice a day—first thing in the morning and before going to bed.

I've made my Power Life Script available as a free resource in PDF and MP4 on: *devonbrough.com/get-ova-it.*

TAKE ACTION!

I've outlined my process above—so why not write your own Power Life Script right now, using my suggestions above or whatever tools you're already comfortable with? Here's a summary of the steps[13]:

- Write by hand or type your story in the present tense.
- Focus on what you want in all the different areas of your life. Give as much detail as possible—include everything.
- Condense, refine and reframe your story in any way that feels good to you.
- See yourself living out this script.
- Read or listen to your script every day, and review things as they occur to you.

Don't think about it—just do it!

This exercise was so powerful. When I listen to the file, I keep my eyes closed and imagine each scene as it unfolds. Over time, this vision has become so etched in my mind that, many times throughout my day, I'll find myself thinking of one of the scenes and smiling.

And it's not just me! A friend of mine was feeling stuck in his career. He couldn't rise any higher in his current position and within his current organisation. I shared this exercise with him, and on my birthday a few months later he sent me a wonderful present: a voice note to say that he'd just landed his dream job in a large global company. He told me he would never have had the courage to leave his old job had I not shared the Power Life Script exercise with him. The process had pushed him to imagine what he really wanted for his life and for his career.

I have no doubt that it will have the same powerful effect in your life.

On his blog, Bob Proctor spells out the benefits of this exercise with these points[14]:

When you write a life script in this manner, it accomplishes five things. It;

- Compels you to change or get very clear on your thoughts about your future;
- Moves you beyond limiting beliefs;
- Keeps you focused on—and, therefore, attracting—what you want rather than what you don't want;
- Intensifies your feelings and expectations about your true desires;
- Harnesses the power of the universe, and attracts people, places and resources just as you want them to be.

I can promise you that if you constantly revisit your script, something within you will stir. Soon you will adopt your vision as the truth—and the more you truly believe it, the more opportunities, encounters and people will be magnetically drawn onto your path to support you.

This is a universal law: what you think about, you bring about.

Chapter 29
Smart Goals

Life punishes the vague wish and rewards the specific ask. After all, conscious thinking is largely asking and answering questions in your own head. If you want confusion and heartache, ask vague questions.
If you want uncommon clarity and results, ask uncommonly clear questions.
– Timothy Ferriss

Please don't move on without completing your Power Life Script, even if it takes you a few days. This is your **vision**—and everything you've worked on so far in the book has been about getting it down on paper. I need you to be crystal-clear on where you're going, so I can show you how to get there when we look at **action** in Part 3.

But… maybe you're still struggling for clarity on your vision. Maybe you're thinking "I want to be happy," but you can't go any deeper than that.

Before learning about SMART goals, I was never very good at drilling down into the details. Because I often lacked clarity, my goals didn't compel me to take action. I've said it before and I'll say it again: you need detail. But I get it—detail is hard! So here's another tool to add to your toolbox.

SMART stands for Specific, Measurable, Attainable, Relevant and Time-bound.[15] This tool simplified my thought processes to ensure that my goals could, in fact, become a reality.

Be Specific

Your goals must be specific. When you say "I want to get in shape" or "I'd like to earn more money," it's not clear what you're really aiming for. Your goals need to be specific.

If you take these two goals and reframe them as follows, you have something to work towards: "I'd like to lose 10 kilograms" and "I'd like to increase my monthly earnings by R20 000."

Having specific goals that are clearly defined means that it's easier to gauge your progress as you move towards them.

Make It Measurable

Making sure that you can measure your goal will help to keep you on track. If you want to lose 10 kilograms and you've given yourself five months to accomplish this, then you can break it down to losing two kilograms every month.

Being able to measure what you need to do is important so that you know whether you're doing well or falling short. If you can't measure your goal, you won't be able to adjust your output during the process.

Make It Attainable

Another word I like to use for "attainable" is "realistic". We often set such massive goals for ourselves that we get stuck before we even start.

If you've never played golf before and battle with hand-eye coordination, setting a goal of becoming a scratch handicap by Christmas is probably a bit far-fetched. But if you set your goal to being able to play a nine-hole course within six months regardless of your score, you have a good chance of attaining it. In the next chapter, we'll discuss how you don't eat an entire elephant in one bite (possibly you don't eat elephant at all, but stay with me on this!). Setting goals that you can comfortably chew on lowers the stress and anxiety that keep you stuck. Being realistic increases motivation as you progress towards your attainable goal.

Make It Relevant

This comes back to being authentic to yourself and making sure you have created a goal that you really want to achieve.

Losing 10 kilograms because your partner thinks you should won't inspire you. Your goal has to come from you. It must be a goal that will bring you joy and excitement when you achieve it. It has to be relevant to *your* life, *your* desires and *your* **vision**.

Make It Time-Bound

If you don't have a time frame attached to your goal, then you won't have a reason to hold yourself accountable to achieving it.

Setting a timeframe is like making a commitment. It will help you track and measure how you are progressing.

TAKE ACTION!

Use SMART goals to review the vision and goals you created for yourself with the Power Life Script. As you chunk down your goals in the next section, you can also check back every time you create a new milestone. Remember to keep your milestones, goals and *vision* SMART!

Chapter 30
Chunking Down

There is only one way to eat an elephant: a bite at a time.
– Archbishop Desmond Tutu

Your dreams may often seem insurmountable if you think of them in a general way. But if you chunk down the task and tackle it one piece at a time, suddenly they become achievable. (And let's face it, if you could actually open your mouth wide enough to eat an elephant in one bite, you'd probably end up with a rib stuck in your throat—so consider it a saving grace that you can't!)

By this point in the book, you'll have given a lot of thought to your dream life and written down a vision for where you want to be. But maybe the journey that lies ahead of you seems so epic that you get stuck in feelings of stress, fear and anxiety when you even think about it. The key here lies in minimising any overwhelming thoughts and feelings by breaking down your vision into manageable goals and milestones.

Let's say you're driving from San Francisco to Los Angeles, which is a 620-kilometre trip that should take about six hours. You want to avoid heavy traffic, so you decide to drive at night when the roads are empty. Here's the thing: in order to drive safely, see potential obstacles and see where you're going, your headlights only need to illuminate about 100 metres ahead of you. Your headlights don't need to illuminate the entire 620-kilometre stretch.

It's the same when it comes to your vision.

The vision you put together in your Power Life Script is your ultimate destination. And the 100-metre stretches of road you see in front of you are the milestones that guide you along the way. The towns you pass are the goals you need to achieve. But if you are going to keep moving, all you ever need to focus on is the next 100 metres, the next milestone. When you get there, you can focus on the next.

It's a long trip—but if you just focus on the stretch of road directly in front of you, you won't get overwhelmed. The next 100 metres are all you need to see, all you need to deal with. It's good to keep your larger vision clear in your mind (so you don't veer off into the Pacific Ocean!), but you don't need to figure out how to navigate every twist and turn in the hundreds of kilometres that lie ahead. That's when you start to feel anxious and overwhelmed.

Just get to the next milestone. When you do that, the goal and ultimately the vision will take care of itself.

The practical process of chunking down is to take your vision and break it up into each area of your life.

TAKE ACTION!

We covered these when we looked at the Wheel of Life in Chapter 23, but here again are the areas to consider:

- Personal growth
- Contribution/charity/volunteering
- Environment
- Recreation/fun
- Romance/love
- Family
- Social/friends
- Health/fitness
- Finance/wealth
- Business/career/studies
- Self-image
- Spirituality

Ask yourself: *When do I want to achieve my dream state in each of these areas?*

Based on your age and where you are in life, the answers to this exercise will be different for every person reading this book. For some aspects, your timeframe may be 20 years; for others, five.

(And just a reminder: your Power Life Script may not be your final destination in life. It's the vision you've set for now, but when you reach that place you'll probably want to stretch yourself to come up with a new vision or destination. This process never stops; your vision should grow and change as you evolve.)

TAKE ACTION!

Let's work through some timeframes. Say you'd like to achieve your *vision* in the next 10 years—that's when you'd like it to be your reality. Ask yourself:

- What's my halfway mark? Where do I need to be in *five* years?
- In order to get there in five years, where do I need to be in *three* years?
- And if I want to reach that point in three years, where do I need to be a year from now?

For each timeframe, map out who you are, what you see around you and what you are doing.

Your one, three and five-year goals should be big goals, like the towns you pass on your road trip. When you reach these places, your life should look quite different from what it looks like right now.

In my last long-term relationship, my girlfriend and I wrote down our own one, three, five and 10-year goals. We cut out pictures that represented these goals, and each created a vision board, which we stuck up inside her dresser. Whenever she came home and complained about having a bad day, we'd walk into the bedroom and open up her dresser. Looking at our dream boards, a smile would come to her face, and I'd remind her of the "5 by 5 rule": "If it's not going to matter in five years, don't waste five minutes thinking about it." That's how we focused on our vision.

TAKE ACTION!

Now that you are looking at where you want to be in a year's time, you can start to zoom in on the detail. Divide up the workload by asking yourself: *What exactly needs to be done every month for the next 12 months?*

To keep track of the details, I suggest you plot out every area of your life on an Excel spreadsheet. Write down your one-year goal in the left-hand column, then work out the monthly milestones you need to achieve in order to get there. The Excel template I use can be downloaded at: *devonbrough.com/get-ova-it.*

At this point, it gets really exciting, because you'll realise that many of these milestones are very simple, absolutely attainable and easily achievable.

If you prefer an even more detailed approach, you can break down your months into weeks, and weeks into days, until you have absolute clarity on what you need to do. One of the many reasons this works so well is because it's really fun to tick off your daily tasks. As you begin to see progress, your motivation and inspiration will skyrocket—motivation that will feed into some of the bigger goals you have set yourself.

In my own life, I began to see that using this method was incredibly rewarding. I started to observe that, in some areas, my one-year goals were being accomplished within a matter of months, while in other areas they took a bit longer to gain traction. There will always be certain areas where you thrive, and others that will take more work.

The magic of having a visual representation like an Excel sheet is that you can see exactly where you are doing well and where you may need to allocate more time and effort. When everything is just in your head, it's a mess. Being able to see your tasks gives clarity, just like the headlights on a car.

Keep going. And whatever you do, don't lose hope.

This is how you eat an elephant one bite at a time.

Chapter 31
Serving Others

Part of being a person is about helping others.
– Regis Murayi

You've got your vision down, and you've checked that your defined goals are what you really want. You've broken it down into achievable parts, and you're raring to go! Before we head into action, I want to share something I've found in my own journey, because maybe it's true for you too.

Nothing brings me more joy and fulfilment than serving others. I've witnessed first-hand that if my goals positively affect other people in some way, support and assistance seem to flood magically onto my path to make them a reality.

So I want to challenge you to become a go-giver instead of just a go-getter. Looking for ways to give back becomes an attitude to live by. How will your life have a positive impact on the world, and how can you continue to contribute to life?

TAKE ACTION!

- As you're setting and reviewing your goals, think of how they could serve others.
- As you plan how your business is going to evolve, how will it serve your employees and the greater community?
- As you advance in your personal growth, how will this add value to your family and friends?
- As you start new hobbies, what positive effect will this have on those close to you?

I live by a simple rule that, in the bank of life, I always want to deposit more than I withdraw. Life is so rich with experiences, opportunities and limitless options to grow, love and succeed. The key is to look for ways to give back and to always leave people and places better off by the energy you have put out.

I truly believe that serving others is our ultimate purpose. If you look back at your goals through this lens, I guarantee that you will find unlimited power that propels you on your journey.

SUMMARY OF VISION

In this section on **Vision,** we've discussed a number of important ideas that will carve out a clear direction and path for you to take in the next section on **Action.**

- Your *vision* is the overall picture of what your future looks like. A clear *vision* will give you a definitive direction to head in so you don't amble around aimlessly in life.
- It helps to create clarity for what you want and who you want to become.
- The Law of Attraction activates your *vision* and magnetically draws it towards you.
- Clarity is powerful, and the more detailed your *vision*, the more it will inspire you to take *action* towards it.
- You need to create balance in your life to be well-rounded.
- The Wheel of Life will help you see where you are out of balance.
- Your values and beliefs will affect your ability to create an empowering *vision*.
- Values are the principles you hold in high regard.
- Beliefs are ideas, assumptions and convictions you hold to be true.
- You can reframe any limiting belief to become an empowering limitless belief.
- Your *vision* has to be authentic and aligned to your true self.
- By feeling the emotions of your future now, you magnetically attract it towards you.
- Writing out a detailed script of your future will create the clear *vision* you need.
- SMART goals help to simplify your goal-setting process.
- Any grand *vision* can be chunked down into smaller bites so you feel more empowered to take *action*.
- When you incorporate serving others into your *vision*, you will find that your cause is supported by the universe and God.

Part 3
Action

Vision without action is merely a dream.
Action without vision just passes the time.
Vision with action can change the world.
– Joel A Barker

This is the final step.

Along this journey, you've taken radical ownership of your past and present. You've reprogrammed your narrative to empower your journey. You've let go of the things that hold you back and don't serve you. You've crafted an epic vision that excites you to the core and gets you up in the morning. Now you're ready to put it all into action.

Every person has great ideas. I'm sure you've dreamed up many businesses and products that could be globally successful. But an idea is just an idea. It's pure potential, a projection in your mind. The missing ingredient is action, and nothing comes to life without it.

Action is what separates the haves from the have-nots. When you start to take action, you start to see results. With action, you begin to move towards your goals.

You start gaining momentum, steady at first, but before you know it, you're experiencing huge breakthroughs and smashing your goals in multiple areas—and ultimately fulfilling your *vision*.

Chapter 32
Where the Rubber Meets the Road

Just remember, you can do anything you set your mind to—but it takes actions, perseverance and facing your fears.
— Gillian Anderson

It's safe to have an idea and a vision. That's just in your head. But taking action is hard. It requires that you expose yourself and your ideas to the world. It requires effort, courage, determination, and perseverance—and often a tough skin.

This is where most people get stuck.

When it comes to taking action, Jim Rohn says that "10% will, 90% won't. The numbers don't change. Only the faces change."[16] Just let that sink in. Only one out of 10 people will take action towards their goals and dreams. Only one out of 10 will get to work to make their vision a reality. And I want to ask you right now—are you that one person? Are you prepared to do whatever it takes to see your vision come to life?

If you've done the work on vision in Part 2, and if it has touched you on a soul level, then I know your answer will be a resounding "YES!"

> "Today I will do what others won't, so tomorrow I can accomplish what others can't."
> — Jerry Rice

You will be the one in 10.

If any part of you is hesitating, I'd like you to read over the content again and dive a bit deeper into the exercises in Part 2. Your vision is the rocket fuel that will move you through the process of taking action, and you need to make sure you have A-grade fuel propelling you throughout this step.

There are four primary barriers that may hold you back from experiencing a breakthrough, and they are all rooted in mindset. They are fear, procrastination (or distraction), people and perfectionism.

These barriers are like trained, lethal killers—like Bradley Cooper in *American Sniper*. They are skilled assassins, crippling your progress, taking out your ideas, goals and dreams one by one. They can keep you in a perpetual holding pattern, stuck in neutral where you feel irritable and frustrated because your life has come to a standstill. In this place, your vision seems like a mere fantasy, not something you have a glimmer of hope in reaching.

The good news is that they can be overcome. You take them out with trained mental agility, so that nothing and no-one will stand in the way of your vision.

We'll disarm those assassins in the next four chapters.

Ready? Let's dig a little deeper.

Chapter 33
Barrier to Action #1: Fear

Fear is stupid. So are regrets.
– Marilyn Monroe

"Fear" is defined as an emotional response to perceived danger. I love that—especially the word "perceived" because, oh boy, can our perceptions be off the mark! In Part 1 we discussed how we can shift and rewrite our perceptions, but let's look at this in a bit more detail.

Fear. When you're walking in the bush and a lion appears out of nowhere, the fear is real. It is physical. That beast could kill you, and it's okay to be afraid. Be very afraid. Because that fear could save your life.

But more often than not, when we encounter fear, we are far from being in a life-threatening situation. We experience fear when we project into the future: when we think about an event, task or even a state of mind that hasn't yet occurred (and may never occur). We fear being alone. We fear feeling inadequate. We fear being judged. We fear being criticised. We fear ridicule.

My biology teacher in high school was also the deputy headmistress. She was an intimidating woman and I was scared of her. One day I hadn't done my homework, but biology was my last class, so I used every free moment in the day to try to get it done. I was in a panic, and I couldn't concentrate in any of my other classes as I replayed the scenes of the ridicule I'd experience if I didn't finish. During both my breaks, I sat writing, missing out on everything going

"Everything you ever wanted is on the other side of fear."

– George Addair

on around me. I managed to finish my homework just before the class started...
Only to find that my biology teacher was absent that day.

What! I'd freaked out the entire day, been engulfed by fear—and she wasn't even there.

The thing is, nine times out of 10, the thing we fear never transpires. That's why I like to call fear a deception rather than a perception. Most fear is a delusion, a lie we keep telling ourselves until we're convinced it's real. It isn't.

I've described previously how for years I'd wanted to write. Why didn't I? Because of my crippling fear of inadequacy. I kept telling myself, What if my content is garbage? What if I'm judged for exposing my alcoholism and drug addiction?

When I published my first blog post and shared it on Facebook, I was terrified that I'd be judged and laughed at. But what actually happened? I received the most amazing messages from friends, family and complete strangers. Everyone was supportive, thankful and even encouraged by my act of vulnerability.

A blog is one thing, but when it came to writing a book, I kept telling myself I just wasn't good enough. Not a single word made it onto a page. I didn't have the guts to even start...

But look what you're holding in your hand right now.

The interesting thing to remember is that we often fear what we most desire—if we didn't care so much, we wouldn't fear the failure of our dreams. In that sense, fear is like a flashing light trying to draw attention to what really matters to us.

> Are you paralysed with fear? That's a good sign. Fear is good. Like self-doubt, fear is an indicator. Fear tells us what we have to do. Remember one rule of thumb: the more scared we are of a work or calling, the more sure we can be that we have to do it.
>
> – Steven Pressfield

What you most fear could just be the thing that will bring you closest to the path of your purpose and your destiny.

TAKE ACTION!

When thinking of the *vision* you've created, what fears come to mind? Now ask yourself these questions:

- Is your fear real or perceived?
- Do you have proof that your fear will materialise?
- What is the cost if you remain stuck in fear, unable to move forward?

Chapter 34
Barrier to Action #2:
Procrastination and Distraction

We'll come back to this topic a bit later—I just need to make coffee and check Instagram… and then I need to call my bestie. Oh look, a WhatsApp…

Procrastination is one of the most common and deadliest of diseases, and its toll on success and happiness is heavy.
– Wayne Gretzky

Guilty as charged.

I used to be a master procrastinator. Many times in my life, it was my biggest stumbling block. So don't be hard on yourself—we all fall victim to procrastination.

According to Vocabulary.com, "Procrastination is putting off or deferring an action (usually one we don't want to do) until a later time (usually the last minute)." Procrastination's cousin is distraction, which "comes from the Latin dis-, meaning 'apart', and trahere, meaning 'drag'." Distraction is when you find yourself being dragged away from your task or from your worries.

> "Procrastination is the thief of time."
>
> – Edward Young

Say no more.

Often, procrastination and distraction are internal triggers to escape discomfort. If you're lonely, you check Facebook. If you're bored, you scroll through Instagram. If you're uncertain, you check out Google or YouTube—and there's always another link to follow, another video to watch, another page to open… What we don't often do is show up for our goals—and ultimately, ourselves.

Procrastination has one simple mission: to divert your time from important tasks that could potentially change your life. Procrastination keeps you busy with menial tasks that have little or no impact on your growth or success. Distraction steals your focus away from the tasks you should be dealing with right now. None of this is helped by the fact that we live in an age of constant distraction when results are expected instantly. We've been conditioned to choose instant gratification over long-term rewards. As we follow celebrities on social media, we see their successes but never their struggles. Millennials, in particular, have an idea in their head that success should come immediately. Let's just say that we're not a generation known for its staying power, and there are plenty of shiny things around us begging for our attention.

The opposite of distraction is traction. So, in a state of distraction you won't build traction towards your desired outcome, which is to move in the direction of your goals and vision. When your attention is continuously diverted to activities that aren't aligned with your goals and purpose, you will begin to experience frustration, stress and anxiety.

When you have a vision that excites you, you won't want to escape. Instead of feeling discomfort, you'll feel excitement as you make progress towards your goals.

TAKE ACTION!

Do a quick audit of your current habits, rituals and routines. Write down:

- How do you procrastinate?
- What non-productive tasks steal your precious time?
- If you minimised time spent on these activities, could your vision become a reality much sooner?

Chapter 35
Barrier to Action #3: People

Confused about this one? I thought so. Yes, people can be a barrier to your breakthrough—even the people closest to you.

Pursuing your gift and expressing your creativity takes something from you that you can never get back—time. And your time is something other people want. Think of the hours it takes to start a new business, study for a new qualification, or practise a craft like writing or playing the guitar. These things don't come easy—and they sure as hell don't come fast.

When you're pursuing your vision, you will often have to choose where to focus your energy and time. Do you go out with your friends, or do you finish that business proposal? Do you spend time on the couch bingeing a series with your partner, or do you work towards those milestones along your journey?

Let's face it, it's way easier to kick back and chill—and often it's a vital ingredient of keeping your life in balance. Having better relationships may even be part of your vision, in which case go for it! But giving birth to something new and exciting almost invariably takes effort, energy and hard work.

> "Nothing that's worthwhile is ever easy. Remember that."
> – Nicholas Sparks

Your partner, your friends and your family naturally want to spend time with you relaxing and having fun, but when you're going through transformative change, you need to allocate your time wisely. This can be especially difficult if you're a people-pleaser (see Chapter 26), and it can be lonely. But short-term sacrifices are critical, and they will be worth it as you evolve into the best version of yourself.

It may be difficult to convince those around you who are asking for your attention that spending less time with them is the right thing to do. If they haven't bought into your vision and don't understand the path you're on, don't be surprised if they actively discourage you. "You're such a dreamer," they might say. Or, "Don't waste your time, you're just setting yourself up for disappointment."

In my experience, I have found that it's often the people who love us the most who discourage us the most. It may not be a malicious action—they may feel as though they're protecting us from the pain or disappointment of not achieving our goals. But sometimes it can come from a selfish space: they need you (to party with, to talk to, to support them) and now you're not there for them. And they may even feel offended by your sudden absence—as though you're judging them by rejecting the part of your life that they used to be more involved in.

Whatever their motivations, you must be protective of your time and energy. If you can get those close to you to understand what you're doing, it will not only explain why you're not spending as much time with them, but it may serve to recruit allies to your cause—fans who will encourage you to do better.

I'm not suggesting that you cast off your friends and family, by any means. Strong relationships are critical to your health and wellbeing, and to your long-term success (and we'll touch on that later). But be careful about who you share your ideas and dreams with. Some people just won't get it, and they may prove to be additional barriers to overcome in achieving your goals.

Protect your vision as though it's the most precious thing you own. Be disciplined about dedicating time to it, and share it in detail only with people who will fan the flames of your passion.

TAKE ACTION!
- Who are the passion killers in your life – those who will dismiss your ideas as foolish or unrealistic?
- Which of your friends divert your attention and coerce you into spending time on activities that don't serve your vision?
- Who will buy into your vision and want to share in your journey with you?

Chapter 36
Barrier to Action #4: Perfectionism

Perfectionism rarely begets perfection, or satisfaction—only disappointment.
– Ryan Holiday

You'd think that perfectionism was a good thing, right? You want to be the best possible version of yourself, or you want to put something out into the world that's as good as it can possibly be—what's wrong with that?

If you scratch below the surface, perfectionism has little to do with the person you're trying to be or the product you want to put out into the world. Perfectionism is actually more about avoiding failure and shielding yourself from being judged by others—two things we can never avoid in life.

Perfectionism is often something we learn in childhood. Our parents want us to be perfect little angels. They push us to get perfect grades, to make the "A" team and to have perfect manners. On a subconscious level, we pick up the limiting belief (see Chapters 24 and 25) that in order to be deserving of love, we have to be, well, perfect. Anything less and we are not deserving. Sadly, perfectionism is driven by fear instead of motivated by love: "If I'm not perfect, then I'm a failure, and then what will people think of me?"

The problem, of course, is that actual perfection isn't an option—as humans, we are almost by definition perfectly imperfect. We're destined to make mistakes, to act on impulse, to fail and to fall short—because it's through trial and error that we grow and learn. That's what makes us human.

The pursuit of perfectionism goes against that. I've said in Part 1 that we grow most through pain, challenges and obstacles and when we're focused on trying to be perfect, we often don't give ourselves permission to even have these experiences. The cult of perfectionism is so pervasive that, when we do make mistakes, we beat ourselves up about them instead of focusing on the lessons and opportunities to grow. When we strive for perfection, we set unachievably high standards for ourselves. Then, when we don't meet them, we become dissatisfied and unhappy, and feel as if we're unworthy and not enough.

> "When Perfectionism is driving, Shame is always riding shotgun – and Fear is the annoying back-seat driver."
> – Brené Brown

In life, the pursuit of perfection will hold you back and keep you stuck. Perfectionists are more prone to procrastination, highly critical and pushed by fear, and they experience heightened feelings of stress and anxiety. Instead of sharing an idea or launching a business, they keep it to themselves, waiting for the perfect moment. (Spoiler alert: there is no perfect moment, so your idea will never see the light of day.)

> "...don't let perfectionism become an excuse for never getting started."
> – Marilu Henner

That isn't the path you should be on. Pursuing your milestones and goals on the road towards your ultimate vision should be fun and exciting. So choose progress over perfection.

I encourage you to celebrate your progress—any and all progress. As long as you're moving forward, as long as you're taking action every single day, that is cause for celebration.

As humans, we connect at the level of our imperfection. We connect with others when we're in a mess, in pain, in stress, in all the areas where we fall short. When you allow yourself to be vulnerable and share your challenges and downfalls, that's when you really connect with another person.

Perfectionism is more robotic, almost fake. The more perfect you try to be, the more you block yourself from experiencing real human connection.

Think of two smooth panes of glass, one on top of the other. Tilt them to the side and the top pane will slide right off—it's so smooth that there are no points of connection, no cohesion. Now, replace the glass with two pieces of sandpaper. The bond is strong because the rough sides stick and hold. As humans, we're like sandpaper—our roughness is what connects us, and it's where we can relate to one another.

One of the ways to counteract your inherent ideal of perfectionism is to foster vulnerability. Being courageous and sharing your difficulties with another human is in complete opposition to the idea of being perfect. You will be amazed at how you will be met with love, compassion, empathy and kindness. And the most beautiful part is that you will never feel alone in the mess.

Be a Beta Person

In the computing industry, products evolve so rapidly that software developers often launch a beta version into the market in order to gain market share and user adoption before a competitor does. A beta version is far from being perfect—it's an early version of an app or a program that is not yet complete. The bugs and faults haven't yet been ironed out. But that's completely fine, because as users adopt and trial the new software, they give feedback that improves the product. The beta version leads to a better version.

Now apply this in your own life.

Think of your Power Life Script—now, instead of waiting for the perfect moment, the perfect product, the perfect you… JUST DO IT! Launch your beta version. Put yourself, your business, your idea or your product out there into the world. It doesn't have to be perfect. It just has to be good enough. Then, as you get real-time feedback, you can tweak until your heart's content. It takes massive courage to launch a brand, business or product; you open yourself up to judgment and sometimes harsh criticism. But nothing ever grew inside a comfort zone. Rather than procrastinating, getting stuck in fear and having nothing to show for it, be courageous and take a leap of faith.

As they say, you have to risk it to get the biscuit!

TAKE ACTION!
- Where in your life do you feel the need to be perfect?
- What progress can you acknowledge yourself to have made since starting this book?
- What beta version are you committing to launch?

Chapter 37
Discipline

Discipline is the bridge between goals and accomplishment.
– Jim Rohn

If there is one quality you need to strive for in order to live a life of success, it's discipline. Discipline is what takes an idea from your mind and produces a tangible result.

In my own life, discipline has been the key ingredient that has always pushed me forward and promoted me to levels I could never have dreamed of. In the industries I've been in, I've never been the most talented person in the room, but I've always been one of the hardest workers, and have always been prepared to learn and put in the hours to hone my craft. It's been my discipline that has enabled me to show up with excellence.

Discipline is the secret sauce—and secret source!

Discipline improves your decision-making abilities, and helps you to make choices that are better for you and more congruent with the goals you've set for yourself.

When I lost 28 kilograms in eight months in my twenties, it was through sheer discipline. Because I'd fostered discipline in my life, I had the ability to say no to delicious food that I loved, but that I knew would take me backwards in achieving my body goals. I could firmly decide between what was good for me and what was bad.

One of my favourite hobbies is show-jumping. I own a horse, Novelty, a 14-year-old chestnut Thoroughbred mare. She's super-feisty and a source of never-ending, unconditional love. Our lessons are always very early in the morning.

Believe me, at 6am in winter, when it's freezing outside, it takes discipline to get out of bed... and on some mornings, I wake up under the warm duvet, feel the cold, see the absolute darkness, and still have moments when I don't feel like getting up. I may be disciplined, but that's perfectly natural.

Remember, our brains work against us here. So my mind starts thinking up excuses, reasons to stay in bed. My head is flooded with thoughts about how uncomfortable it will be at the stable this early.

But then discipline kicks in, and I get my mind in check. I'm not a quitter, I take accountability and I don't make excuses. Discipline gets me out of bed and helps me overrule the feelings that would rather keep me comfortable—and stuck.

Can you relate to this? Have you ever had something difficult or uncomfortable to do and your own mind talked you out of it? If you've honed the skill of discipline, it becomes easier and easier to do the things that need to get done—even if they are tough.

> "We must all suffer one of two things: the pain of discipline or the pain of regret and disappointment."
>
> – Jim Rohn

Discipline is the process of conquering self. It takes your "I could" and "I should" and turns them into "I must" and "I will".

One of my favourite books, by author and speaker Brian Tracy, is *No Excuses! The Power of Self-Discipline*. There are so many truths in this book, one of which is that while people may think success comes from luck or talent, successful people are actually those who display self-discipline.

As I started to incorporate these teachings into my life, I saw the effects multiply. Discipline touches every single area of your life: career, finances, health, fitness and relationships. Absolutely no area is immune from the effects of the powerful quality of discipline.

For me, the discipline I've applied to getting fit shows in the love I now have for my body. I used to be overweight and ashamed, but now my body is strong and fuelled by energy, which helps me work optimally throughout the day. Because I have a great relationship with my body, I now feel confident in many other areas of my life too.

If you asked the question, "When is the best time to take action?" The answer would be "Immediately." There's a huge amount of energy in the moment you make a decision. Discipline captures that energy and channels it into action.

This energy builds, and as you take more action, you pick up more momentum. Soon you're taking action on autopilot—it's no longer a chore, and you make simple, light work of any task. This is how you zoom past your milestones and towards your goals.

Discipline also has powerful side effects. It builds your self-worth and value. Conversely, a lack of discipline can break down your self-worth and sense of personal value. One of the pillars of self-worth is how you show up for yourself. When you lack discipline and don't do what you say you're going to do, you create a negative self-belief that you are unreliable or even useless, and cannot show up for yourself. This can awaken feelings of guilt and shame, and a toxic cycle of self-judgment.

Discipline counteracts this. As you grow your discipline, your self-worth will increase. Knowing that you will actually take action after you've made a decision is incredibly powerful. Being able to truly rely on your own word puts you in a powerful position to make things happen.

And it's people who make things happen who change the world.

Everything Matters

When it comes to discipline, absolutely everything matters. You may think letting yourself off the hook with something small doesn't make a difference, but it really does. You're not cheating anyone other than yourself.

Let's say you've committed to a diet, and you've been going strong for a few days. In a moment of craving, you spot your favourite chocolate in the aisle of temptation at the supermarket and you decide you have to have it. "Hey, it's just one chocolate," your brain will rationalise. "It doesn't matter." But if being disciplined takes you one step forward, a lack of discipline sets you three steps back.

Immediately after eating the chocolate, your inner voice will tell you that it wasn't the right decision. As your guilt rises, you can either catch yourself and get back on track, or you can allow yourself to spiral right out of control, continuing the destructive pattern.

The self-compassionate response is to say, "Hey, I made a mistake. I'm human. I'm going to be kind to myself and re-commit." Then you can get back on the train. This would be an empowering way to handle a small slip-up.

But often we are so conditioned to be our own worst critic that a completely different scenario plays out. After eating the chocolate, your inner voice sounds like this: "Damn, I'm stupid. I don't have any willpower; I can't even stick to a simple diet." In that moment, you become your own policeman, judge and executioner—and to punish yourself, you spend the rest of the day binge-eating just to show yourself how bad you really are.

This disempowered approach keeps you stuck in harsh, critical self-judgment. Eating the chocolate itself isn't that bad, but the act of doing it can be devastating, playing tricks on your mind, and preventing you from picking yourself up and getting back on your way to your goal.

When you falter, it's important to acknowledge your humanity, to be kind to yourself, to show self-compassion and to gently motivate yourself back into positive action.

But as much as possible, stay disciplined!

TAKE ACTION!
- Where do you lack discipline in your life?
- Which of your habits work against you when it comes to achieving your goals?

Chapter 38
Personal Integrity

Integrity is the practice of being honest and showing a consistent and uncompromising adherence to strong moral and ethical principles and values. In ethics, integrity is regarded as the honesty and truthfulness or accuracy of one's actions.

– Wikipedia

Integrity is made up of a number of principles. For me, the most important principles that fall under this umbrella are honesty, respect, reliability and consistency. Personal integrity is when you adhere to these qualities for yourself, in all that you do—especially when no-one's watching.

Yet we often put ourselves in positions where these qualities are compromised—and with them, our self-worth. As humans, most of us have fallen into a pattern of lying to ourselves, continuously reinforcing the self-belief that we are not capable of showing up for ourselves. And when you truly believe that you're not capable of showing up for yourself, you're unlikely to even start the journey towards your goals. This can be devastating to your psyche.

The Snooze Buttons

I love using this example because it's something we can all relate to. I know you've woken up some mornings and just haven't felt like getting out of bed. You hit that snooze button—"Come on, it's just 10 more minutes." Maybe you do it every morning. Maybe you have five, six, even 10 alarms set. Let me tell you why this is so destructive.

Before you go to bed the previous night, you've set an intention (in the form of your alarm) to wake up at a specific time. From a psychological point of view, you've made a commitment to yourself and have defined the time that you intend to wake up.

But as your alarm sounds in the morning, you reach over and, in what seems like a small gesture, you hit snooze. What you've really done—before the day has even started—is broken a promise to yourself.

Say what! Yes, you've just shown that the intention you set the night before means nothing to you. You've just told yourself that your intentions carry no weight and don't matter. You set a commitment and an intention, but when you needed to step up to execute, you couldn't follow through.

Sounds harsh, right? But this is the subconscious loop that has just been triggered.

If you rarely do this—perhaps only on weekends when you don't have set commitments—don't be so hard on yourself. But if this is the norm for you, be aware that you have created an internal feedback loop that says, "I cannot show up for myself. If I set an intention, I cannot rely on myself to follow through."

If this is your inner dialogue, do you think you'll be inspired to start a business, knowing the amount of work and commitment it takes? Will you be able to stand up for yourself in a romantic relationship by having difficult conversations? Will you feel inspired to take action towards your goals?

Internally, you will have created the expectation that if you can't show up for yourself when it comes to simple things like getting out of bed, you won't have the motivation and determination to tackle the big tasks. And how can you then trust yourself to act on the bigger decisions and commitments?

It's how we show up in the little things that determines how we act with the big things. Get the little things right and the bigger things will fall into place.

TAKE ACTION!
- Where in your life do you constantly break little promises to yourself?
- How do you feel when you cannot rely on yourself?
- How would you feel if you absolutely knew you *could* rely on yourself?

Chapter 39
Start Small

Greatness comes by doing a few small and smart things each and every day.
Comes from taking little steps, consistently. Comes from making a few small
chips against everything in your professional and personal life that is ordinary,
so that a day eventually arrives when all that's left is the Extraordinary.
– Robin Sharma

If you're now completely guilt-ridden thinking about your intimate relationship with the snooze button, don't be rash—put down that knife. There's still hope!

As with building any quality, when it comes to building personal integrity and discipline, it's all about starting small.

I may be disciplined, but patience has never been a strong quality of mine. When I want something, I want it now. It's an area I'm constantly working on.

Growth is about taking lots of small actions which, when stacked together over a period of time, add up to create change. We may live in a time of instant gratification, but we need to let go of the idea that growth is instant or fast, because it really isn't. Decisions can be made in an instant, but it takes time to craft and execute an action plan.

For a while I wanted to call this book Explosive Breakthrough. The title sounded powerful, but it ultimately didn't sit well with me, because growth is not explosive. We may all want instant results, but true growth is gradual—and gradual growth is something that lasts.

It's critical to realise that true growth often starts slowly and almost imperceptibly. You become aware that a certain behaviour pattern isn't serving you. You read a book, listen to a few podcasts. You come across a new idea that piques your interest. Then, like going on a first date, you find yourself thinking a lot about this new idea. You hold its hand and slowly get used to it. When you're comfortable with it, you start making it part of your life. You mould it, make it your own, tweak it to fit your reality. Then you teach it to someone else.

Growing self-discipline is a slow, gradual process. We discussed in Chapter 30 that you cannot eat an elephant in one bite; it needs to be chunked down into manageable portions. Building discipline is much the same, just in reverse: instead of chunking down, you're building up.

Bit by bit, a little adds up to a lot. If you feel like you're lacking self-discipline, you may feel compelled to make a list of 20 areas in your life where you should be more disciplined, all at once. But biting off more than you can chew will set you up for failure.

TAKE ACTION!

To build discipline in any area, choose *one* task where you'd like to be more disciplined. Practise this task consistently until it has become a habit.

Most experts say that it takes 21 days (three weeks) for a behaviour to become a habit, and 66 days (three months) for it to become automatic, where you no longer have to think about it.

It will be difficult at first—your brain will constantly fight you as it seeks to stay in a known, familiar pattern. But as you progress, it becomes easier. Before you know it, you'll have hardwired a new habit that eventually runs on autopilot.

One new habit at a time—that's how you build discipline.

Waking up at a set time, getting to gym four times a week, cooking healthy meals for dinner instead of eating out, phoning your mom every few days, reading for 30 minutes or listening to an audiobook before bed—whatever the habit is, one by one, you'll begin to create excellence in your life.

> "Daily ripples of excellence—over time—become a tsunami of success."
> – Robin Sharma

THE POWER OF ONE-CENT DECISIONS

To get a real sense of how small actions stack up over time, imagine this scenario. I have a duffel bag with R3-million in cold, hard cash. You can take the money right now—or I'll put one cent aside for you and I'll keep doubling the amount every day for a full calendar month of 31 days.[17]

So, which option will you take?

Let me show you what happens if you take the one-cent option.

Day 1: R0.01
Day 2: R0.02
Day 3: R0.04
Day 4: R0.08
Day 5: R0.16
Day 6: R0.32
Day 7: R0.64
Day 8: R1.28
Day 9: R2.56
Day 10: R5.12

Hmm, by Day 10 it's not looking great—only R5.12? Not convinced, right? But let's keep going.

Day 11: R10.24
Day 12: R20.48
Day 13: R40.96
Day 14: R81.92
Day 15: R163.84
Day 16: R327.68
Day 17: R655.36
Day 18: R1 310.72
Day 19: R2 621.44
Day 20: R5 242.88

By Day 20, I've got R5 242.88 for you—you must be so frustrated! You're two-thirds of the way in and you've barely made a dent in the R3-million...

Day 21: R10 485.76
Day 22: R20 971.52
Day 23: R41 943.04
Day 24: R83 886.08
Day 25: R167 772.16
Day 26: R335 544.32
Day 27: R671 088.64
Day 28: R1 342 177.28
Day 29: R2 684 354.56
Day 30: R5 368 709.12
Day 31: R10 737 418.24

On Day 25, you break six figures with R167 772.16 – still negligible compared to the R3-million you could have had, but things are moving fast. By Day 28 you break the seven-figure mark with R1 342 177.28 – a definite improvement! It's at Day 30 that you suddenly realise being patient has paid off. You're at R5 368 709.12 – almost double what you would've settled for. To top it off, on Day 31 you receive your final payout of R10 737 418.24 – a whopping three times what you would've received had you chosen instant gratification on Day 1.

What does this show you?

The long tail pays off. A one-cent decision, multiplied each day, is more effective than an instant win – exponentially so. Yet many people lose hope and throw in the towel before they reach the payout point.

It's persistence and patience that get the goods—yet often, when someone starts a business, launches a service or begins to unleash an idea into the world, they lose hope and give up because they don't see an instant result. Yes, it's hard. Yes, it takes courage. Yes, it requires discipline. But the end result is so worth it.

"Our greatest weakness lies in giving up. The most certain way to succeed is always to try just one more time."

– Thomas Edison

Do not give up on yourself. Do not give up on your vision or the life you are so worthy and deserving of. Commit to staying the course.

The one-cent analogy can be applied to every area of your life, especially personal growth. Start making one-cent decisions that move you forward, and one day you'll look back and not recognise how far you've come.

Imagine you are climbing a mountain. You start out in the morning with tons of energy, and you're excited to see the incredible views from the top. But the

"Being defeated is often a temporary condition. Giving up is what makes it permanent."

— Marilyn vos Savant

day wears on and you climb for hours, and the peak is still not in sight. Now it's late afternoon and the sun starts to dip. You're tired. You keep pushing, but the light is fading and you know it's dangerous to summit in the dark.

Exhausted and at the point of wanting to give up, you see someone coming towards you. As they pass, they say, "Hey, you're almost there. The summit is just around the next corner." Now wouldn't that inspire you? You'd have a newfound sense of excitement and you'd find the energy to push through.

Had that person not appeared, perhaps you would've given up, turned back and never experienced the glorious views from the top of the mountain. And isn't this what happens in life?

My message to you is simple: Do not give up!

At any point in time, you may be just inches from reaching your goal. Nothing in life is certain. We cannot control what happens outside of us. But this much is guaranteed: if you give up, you will not experience your breakthrough, you will not meet the best version of yourself, and you definitely will not make your vision a reality.

You are so worthy and deserving. Commit to making one-cent decisions daily, taking one step at a time towards the life of your dreams. And whatever you do, do not give up.

TAKE ACTION!
- What are the one-cent decisions you can begin to make in your life?
- Over a period of time, what effect will these have on your life and state of mind?
- What will it cost you if you give up before you receive your payoff?

Chapter 40
Strike When the Idea Is Hot!

The longer you wait to do something you should do now, the greater the odds that you will never actually do it.
– John C Maxwell

In my workshops, I often get asked when the best time is to start taking action. It's simple: the best time to take action is right away, before the feeling of inspiration and excitement passes.

Jim Rohn, who was Tony Robbins's mentor and an incredible teacher of life, speaks about the Law of Diminishing Intent: how our intention diminishes the longer we wait to take action. He says, "Here is the time to act: when the idea is hot and the emotion is strong."[18]

There's so much energy stored in the moment that you make any decision. As time passes, the energy potential diminishes.

The more time passes, the less likely you are to take any action at all.

We intend to do something when the idea strikes us and when inspiration is high. But if you don't translate that into action fairly soon, then the intent diminishes. A month from now, it's cold. A year from now, it's disappeared.
– Jim Rohn

You have to take action immediately. Action creates momentum, and when you harness the power of momentum, it becomes easier to take even more action.

Think of pedalling a bicycle. From standstill, the first few pushes are the hardest. But once the wheels are in motion, it becomes easier to pick up speed—

you can shift up a gear, and you need less energy to keep the bike moving. It's the same with taking action in any area of your life. Starting is always the hardest part, but once you've gained momentum from even the smallest actions, you're in motion. As you increase your speed, it soon feels like you're flying towards your goals.

While you have the power of momentum, your excitement and motivation are high. When you encounter an obstacle in the road, you don't need to come to a standstill. Remember the lessons from Part 1—if it's out of your control, change your perspective, attach a new meaning and keep pedalling.

Keep going, no matter what.

Chapter 41
Comfort Vs Calling

Life begins at the end of your comfort zone.
– Neale Donald Walsch

You can have comfort or you can have a calling, but you can't have both. Your comfort zone is the thief of your dreams. I want to challenge you to start finding comfort in discomfort...

Wait. What does that even mean?

It takes immense courage to leave what's known and familiar. Breaking your routine so you can start taking new action in different areas of your life is scary. Remember, your brain wants to keep you safe, and safety means staying in the familiar—even if that doesn't push you to grow, or make you happy in the long term.

Your goals most likely involve you doing a lot of things you may not yet be comfortable with: meeting new people, making calls to strangers, engaging in activities you know nothing about, learning and growing new skills. This takes courage and effort. It would be easier to just settle for where you are—coming home at the end of every day, putting your feet up and turning on your favourite Netflix series.

But that's not going to get you anywhere.

The good news is that it's in discomfort that you begin to experience progress and growth. As your life starts to change for the better, you feel positive and excited for each new day. Then you begin to actively seek discomfort, because you know it heralds more breakthrough and growth. Amid the obstacles and challenges you face as you move towards your purpose, comfort is in the pursuit of your calling.

For me, whenever I feel comfortable, I know I'm not pushing myself hard enough. Sure, you need to find balance—and you also need time to switch off, rest, recuperate and unwind. But when it's grind time, I like to push myself, and give myself tasks that will stretch my abilities and skills. When I feel like a task will push me outside of my comfort zone, that's when I know I need to do it.

In February 2021, I decided to run my first Breakthrough Workshop. I'd been talking about it for a while with close friends, but I hadn't taken any action yet. One Sunday evening I noticed that I was getting irritated with myself, because I knew I was procrastinating instead of getting my workshops off the ground. The idea was hot in my mind, so right there and then I found a free design website that has hundreds of templates for adverts that require no graphic-design experience to use; in other words, there was no excuse for why I couldn't move forward. (If you don't know it, it's called Canva.com—and you're welcome!)

In an hour I'd put together my first advert:

I'd committed to a date that was just two weeks away, and although I knew what I wanted to teach, I hadn't even put together the course outline or agenda. I'm very aware of what makes me tick—I thrive on pressure. Two weeks gave me just enough time to get this done while creating the pressure that would get me excited to do the work.

I put the ad out on my Instagram account with a short description of what I'd be teaching. To my amazement, I woke up the next morning to six enquiries in my inbox. I sent out a more comprehensive emailer with additional details and the content breakdown for the day, and within 48 hours four people had registered and made electronic transfers into my bank account.

I couldn't back out now; I had to make it happen.

Two weeks later, I held my first Breakthrough Workshop with the original four respondents and two friends I'd invited to join for free so they could give me honest feedback. The day was a huge success, and driving home I felt a great sense of pride and gratitude. I'd just proved to myself that I could hold an audience for an entire day—eight full hours of speaking and teaching was something I'd never done before.

Was it out of my comfort zone? Absolutely. But I knew this work was part of my calling.

I got home and, while still on the energetic high from the day, I set the next workshop date for one month away. By the time that day came, I had a sponsor and 20 clients—I'd more than tripled the number of attendees in a single month.

The momentum continued, and by June I was running a Breakthrough Workshop and two Relationship Mastery Workshops. I capped the number of attendees at 15 for each event to allow people time to share their stories. My events have been fully booked ever since, and I truly believe that the content is making a difference in people's lives.

Action is what turned an idea in my mind into reality. These workshops serve so many people while generating substantial revenue, and growing my brand and a following for the work I do.

The book you are reading right now has materialised out of the workshops.

So, what would've happened had I not stepped out of my comfort zone and taken action back in February 2021, when the idea was burning in my mind? What if I'd decided to just order takeaways and switch on Netflix?

Nothing would have happened. Not the workshops, not the secondary income—and you would not be reading this book.

It all starts when you take action in the heat of the moment, when the idea is hot and your desire to execute is high. One action—just one moment of stepping outside your comfort zone in the direction of your calling—can start a ripple of change across your whole life.

The only question is, how badly do you want it?

Paying the Price

Maybe you've seen Grant Cardone on Instagram, or in the adverts for the "10X Growth Conference" he hosts for thousands of people in sold-out events across the US.[19]

Grant is the youngest of five siblings. He had a tumultuous upbringing and was raised by a single mother after his father died when he was just 10 years old. Having battled drug addiction, Grant decided to turn his life around at the age of 25. His success began in the car-sales industry, where he broke multiple sales records. He became obsessed with success and went on to create his own sales consultancy.

Today, Grant is an international speaker, the author of many bestselling books, and the founder of the 10X movement. As someone who works in property, I'm particularly interested in his real-estate portfolio: he's grown it to a value of nearly $2-billion.

Grant flies around the world with his family in his branded Gulfstream jet, and truly lives his brand.

One piece of advice stands out for me: "Pay the price today, so you can pay any price tomorrow." This is what it means to choose your calling over comfort: temporarily sacrificing comforts for the delayed gratification of living in alignment with your calling.

Chapter 42
Pain Vs Pleasure

Let's dive a bit deeper into neurobiology, the study of how your brain works.

It's been scientifically proven that your brain will always move towards pleasure and away from pain. This is because your brain's primary purpose is to keep you safe. What feels good and pleasurable is considered safe, and what feels painful is considered unsafe or threatening.

In the process of moving towards our goals, this poses a major problem: it's uncomfortable, and sometimes even painful, to take action in a new and unfamiliar direction. Sometimes, in order to make progress, you need to literally fight your brain and your own thinking. It's the same when it comes to taking action. Have you ever noticed how your thoughts, the language of your brain, will try to convince you to avoid doing uncomfortable or painful things? Conversely, your thoughts may even encourage you to do things that are bad for you—just because they're familiar.

To illustrate this rather fascinating phenomenon, here are two examples.

On a weekday evening after a heavy weights session at gym, I love taking a 20-minute steam session or sauna. The heat relaxes me and eases the aches in my muscles.

For many years, I'd read about the benefits of having an ice bath straight after a sauna, and how cold therapy improves your immune system and cardiovascular circulation, is brilliant for your lymphatic system, and elevates your level of happiness. Tony Robbins, the ultimate self-help guru, raves about cold-water therapy: every morning, he gets into a pool that's cooled to 14°C. And if Tony does it, I want to do it too. The problem is, for years, as I left the sauna or steam room, my mental chatter would kick in:

"What? Are you crazy?"

"This is going to hurt."

"You don't need to do this."

"You can start tomorrow…"

For so long, I listened to my thoughts and avoided the discomfort. My thoughts ruled my actions. I couldn't have what I really wanted because I was weaker than my own thinking.

Then I read Mel Robbins's book *The 5 Second Rule*, in which she shares how she used to battle to get out of bed in the morning. Within seconds of making a decision, our brain tries to talk us out of it, so her method—as we saw in Chapter 7—is to give yourself a countdown, just like they do when launching a rocket into space: 5-4-3-2-1. As you pass "1", you launch into action.

"Right, I'm doing it!" I said to myself as I got out of the sauna one evening. Enough was enough—I was sick and tired of letting my thoughts have free rein over me. I'd take back control.

I marched towards the shower. The mental chatter started immediately, louder than it had ever been. I remember saying to my mind under my breath, "You're not the boss of me."

I turned the mixer to the coldest setting, hesitated for a second, and then pushed the button that fired off the jet of freezing water.

I lasted for all of 20 seconds. The water felt like needles on my skin. But I didn't care. Dancing around like a monkey and making weird gasping sounds, I switched off the water and grabbed my towel. I'd finally done it. It was a victory.

I had stood up to my own thoughts and shown them who was boss.

The trick with any new habit is repetition, so I continued this ritual every time I had a sauna. I made sure to do it every single day, because I wanted it to become a habit that would stick. In the first week, the voices in my head actually got louder—my brain seemed to know that I'd mounted an attack against it, that I'd become stubborn and noncompliant. But I continued to defy my own thinking, and finally the voices started getting quieter, until eventually they were gone.

A fortnight in and I had no problem standing under a cold shower for up to two minutes, allowing my body temperature to drop so the benefits could kick in. The dancing and weird sounds stopped and I felt so alive. Today, taking a cold shower is a habit one that I cannot go a day without, summer or winter.

Another example is when I wanted to start losing weight. I'd make it through a few days in a row sticking to my diet. I'd prep and cook healthy meals, and I would feel a real sense of accomplishment when I stuck to my eating plan. I knew this would lead me to achieving my dream body. This was so important to me because for many years I'd hated the way I looked.

Then one evening after gym, I drove past my favourite fast-food chain and my thoughts started to run wild:

"Come on, treat yourself."

"One burger won't even touch sides."

"You've been so good, reward yourself…"

I drove into the parking lot, but I just sat in my car. See, after the cold-shower experience, I knew I just needed a moment for the chatter to die down. In fact, I used the opportunity to record a video on exactly this topic in the moment: how my own thinking was trying to sabotage my efforts and didn't actually support my vision for a better body. My thoughts wanted to lure me to the immediate comfort of a dopamine rush.

I know that if I didn't have the foresight to just sit with my thoughts for a minute that night, I probably would've had a burger. Actually, two burgers, chips and a fizzy drink—because, hey, I don't do half measures.

It's crucial to realise that you are not your mind or your body. Your thoughts are powerful, and they can steer you away from your goals, your vision and your dreams. They can talk you out of doing what's good for you and into doing what's bad for you.

Bob Proctor and Joe Dispenza speak a lot about the fact that you are the observer behind your thoughts, and that your body is merely the vehicle you use to navigate through your life. You think thousands of thoughts every day—some positive, some negative—but you don't change as fast as your thoughts do, so you are not your thoughts.

As the observer, you are consciousness, pure awareness of your body and your thoughts. The beauty is that you can choose which thoughts to accept and which to reject.

To take action, you need to teach yourself that you are more powerful than your thoughts. You need to train yourself to reject thoughts that do not support your vision.

Every time you go against your own thinking and take action that is challenging, you get stronger. You affirm yourself every time you don't listen or act on thoughts that are not aligned with the direction of your goals and vision. Slowly but surely, as I did with the cold shower, you need to show yourself that you can stay in authentic alignment with your highest vision of yourself, that your desire to achieve your vision is more important than the voices in your head.

Let's face it, those voices will never go away—but they *can* be quietened with time and become easier to overrule. Ultimately, you are in control of the *action* you choose to take. Nothing can lead you off course unless you allow it.

As you take control of your brain and your own thinking, you become the captain of your life and master of your own destiny. You can steer the ship in any direction you want to—and as you aim towards your vision, you will see how fun it becomes to smash goal after goal.

TAKE ACTION!

Take a moment and think where your thoughts sabotage your progress or prevent you from taking any *action* at all.

- What thoughts hold you back from activities that are good for you?
- What thoughts convince you to pursue activities that are bad for you?
- How does this make you feel?

Chapter 43
Peak Performance Habits

[peek per-fawr-muh-ns]
A state in which a person is in the zone of optimal creation, productivity, focus,
health, love, joy and flow. It is in this state that individuals create
extraordinary results, able to radically change their lives… and even the
world.
– Adam Siddiq

I hope it's become evident that the more peak performance habits you adopt, the easier it becomes to take *action* every day. If you know the formula for creating a habit (go back to Chapter 39 for a refresher, or think of me having a daily cold shower!), you'll be able to take willpower out of the equation, and will soon be able to rely on the momentum of the habits you have built to get the results you are after.

"Remember, every professional was once an amateur, and every master started as a beginner. Ordinary people can accomplish extraordinary feats, once they've routinised the right habits."

– Robin Sharma

Robin Sharma says that excellence is not something you just wake up to; excellence is created by the sum of the habits, rituals and routines you have set up in your life.

In other words, to perform at your peak, you have to cultivate healthy behaviours in your body, mind and soul.

When I came out of rehab, I knew my future would be greatly affected by the quality of the new habits and routines that I had begun to set up. Tim Ferriss's books *Tools of Titans* and *Tribe of Mentors* were both invaluable, as they contain a compilation of tools, tactics and habits from more than 130 of the world's top achievers. I also loved Robin Sharma's The *5AM Club*, which helps you master your morning and set up the habits, rituals and routines that will place you on a path of excellence.

I know there have been lots of ideas in this book, but transformation really does come down to the actions you take every day, little by little—because it's the accumulation of the smallest moments that can make the biggest changes.

In the next three chapters, we'll look more closely at the habits you should cultivate in the three main areas of your life: your body, mind and soul.

Chapter 44
Peak Performance Habits for Your Body

Take care of your body.
It's the only place you have to live.
– Jim Rohn

Your body is an incredible piece of machinery. When it's healthy, it functions without you ever needing to think about it. Your heart beats more than 100 000 times each day. If you stretched out your blood vessels, you could wrap them around the entire planet four times. And how mind-blowing is it that 25-million new cells are produced every single second?

Your body is a miracle machine. It is God's highest creation... but you only have one. So the first area of peak performance is to ensure that you keep your body in tip-top condition.

What follows are some habits that I have adopted and would recommend as solid guidelines to support your success. These habits will ensure that you have optimal energy to face your day feeling fit, confident and strong as you go to work fulfilling your goals.

Get Enough Sleep

The science on this is settled: a good night's sleep makes a profound difference in your all-round health and functionality. Seven to eight hours is the recommended amount of sleep for an adult, so be sure to get it. If you think you're doing fine on four hours, or you struggle to sleep, read one of the many good books on the subject, such as *Why We Sleep* by Matthew Walker.

Your circadian rhythm is your body's natural clock, a cycle it likes to stick to. It's incredibly beneficial for your body if you keep to the same bed and wake-up times every day, even during the weekend. Late nights throw your circadian rhythm out of sync, and it takes time to adjust and recalibrate.

"According to NASA, a 26-minute power nap improves performance by 34% and alertness by 54%. Can't squeeze in 26 minutes? Even 15 minutes will do your body good."

– Natalie Ledwell

I get into bed every night at about 8.30pm and wake up at 4.30am. When I can, I take a 30-minute nap during the day, at about 3pm, to give me loads of energy for my evening routine, which includes weight training, writing and reading. Blue light from computer and cell phone screens excites your brain and keeps it in an alert state. For a good night's rest, be sure to limit your exposure for at least an hour before going to sleep. A dark, cool room free from noise and distractions is the optimal setting to get good-quality rest.

Exercise

Aside from being good for your heart, increasing your blood flow and enhancing your circulation, regular exercise has so many other benefits.

I exercise twice a day. My cardio or aerobic exercise comes early in the morning in the form of riding my horse—yes, keeping my 400-kilogram chestnut Thoroughbred mare going around a track and over jumps works up quite a sweat! And it's the connection with this beautiful animal that I just love.

Then, after a busy workday, I do weight training at around 5pm. This is a decompression session for me—any stress that has built up from the day is released as I tackle the heavy weights. I have a personal trainer three evenings a week and train by myself for three more, for a total of six days a week.

Weight training engages both my body and my mind, and it's so rewarding to push my body beyond my personal bests. Watching my body transform creates immense confidence, which filters into every area of my life.

Another amazing benefit of training in the evening is that, when I get into bed, my body is tired and I fall asleep quickly, without any need for artificial assistance like sleeping tablets.

The discipline I apply to my training creates discipline in other areas. The most amazing benefit is that looking into the mirror and feeling genuinely happy in my body fosters self-love and acceptance.

Drink Water and Eat Well

It's so important to stay hydrated. Your body is continuously flushing out toxins, and needs water to maintain its metabolic and maintenance processes. Having optimal hydration aids digestion, regulates body temperature, creates saliva, promotes weight loss, helps with the absorption of nutrients and increases energy. When you're not drinking enough water, you may feel aches and pains, have persistent headaches, or feel lethargic and tired. You may even slow down your bowel function, feel dizzy and get muscle cramps.

Stay away from carbonated drinks and excessive alcohol. Carbonated drinks often contain high volumes of sugar, which also causes dehydration. Alcohol is toxic to your body and messes with your brain function—which is why we call it being intoxicated. You cannot expect to operate at your peak if you're bingeing on alcohol. Also, if you're a big coffee drinker, have a glass of water between cups, as caffeine also promotes dehydration.

When it comes to eating, I encourage you to examine your habits. Look at it this way: if you drove a Ferrari, you wouldn't use substandard petrol or oil in it. To keep this powerful, highly specified and fine-tuned motor in top form, wouldn't you want to only use the cleanest high-performance fuels and lubricants?

I recommend you treat your body in the same way.

I love eating clean. Sure, I create space on a Sunday to "cheat" when I'm not strict about what I eat. But Monday to Saturday, I stick to a healthy menu of meals. No excuses.

When I say clean, what do I mean? For protein, I eat eggs, chicken, red meat, fish and protein powders. My carbohydrates are oats, rice, sweet potato and green vegetables. I get healthy fats from unsweetened peanut butter.

As a rule of thumb, I avoid all processed food. The more processed, the more artificial ingredients have gone into the food, so I try to stay as close as possible to food that is "from farm to table". During the week I steer away from all sugars, all breads, fried food, processed dairy, sugary drinks, chocolates and anything that's been sweetened.

If you start to hydrate and eat well, you'll be amazed at how your body will show up for you. Your body is a pure energy-producing machine, which is what you need to tackle your goals. Make healthy choices and help your body carry you through this journey of life. Remember: it's the only one you have.

Rest

What! I can't rest. I have goals to achieve, and an epic vision to realise!

If these are your first thoughts when you read the word "rest", and if you're thinking "I'll rest when I'm dead," then you and I are very similar. As peak performers, we have a tendency to push ourselves as hard as we can. But if we spend long periods of time at full throttle, we risk hitting a wall.

This was a really difficult concept for me to grasp. Alcoholism and addiction come with one quality that can be both a blessing and a curse: obsession. When I set my mind to a task, I go all in. In small doses this is good, but when it prohibits you from taking time off and resting, it can be detrimental, and can even lead to burnout. Not getting enough rest can have a profound impact on cognitive processes, like your memory and mood.

Take one day a week to rest—that's all I'm asking. A regular, set period of rest and relaxation doesn't just prevent burnout; it actually improves your ability to work. It sharpens your creativity,
problem-solving abilities and focus. Rest recharges your internal batteries, which helps you to show up with excellence and renewed productivity. Rest rejuvenates the body, mind and soul. Rest also improves your happiness, and getting ample rest reduces stress, anxiety and mental fatigue.

Rest is different from sleep. It's when you consciously choose to unplug from the world, come back to yourself, go within or calmly connect with others. It's something I really battled with at first. My internal critic would say, "Hey, you've got so much to do! Don't take your foot off the gas. What have you done to earn a rest?" You need to silence this inner critic that wants to keep you working 24/7.

I've made Sunday my day. Saturdays are always busy, especially in property, with people wanting to view new homes. But on Sundays I don't make any plans, so that I can do whatever I feel like doing, and I choose activities that are good for my soul. If I want to stay home to watch YouTube or read, I do that. Sunday is my day.

And, oh boy, I wake up on Monday excited and energised, and ready for a week of action!

Chapter 45
Peak Performance Habits for Your Mind

Your mind is the soil that grows your thoughts. It's where your dreams and imagination develop, and where meaning is made. The better you tend to this soil, the more fertile it will be, and the richer your harvest. In the same way, your body responds to what you feed it, your state of mind is determined by what you put in.

> "Ships don't sink because of the water around them; ships sink because of the water that gets in them. Don't let what's happening around you get inside you and weigh you down."
>
> – Unknown

If you don't cultivate healthy habits of mind, you leave yourself unprotected—to news that triggers fear and anxiety, gossip that distracts you from your goals, mindless social media that enables procrastination… An unguarded mind will keep you stuck and prevent you from moving forward.

The following peak performance habits are like fertiliser for the garden of your mind. Creating a state of peace, calm, love, optimism and gratitude will enrich you, and exponentially increase your cognitive abilities, creativity, productivity and mental output. When you remain razor-focused on your goals, your mind becomes your greatest asset, generating endless strategies and solutions to help you take action. This is what you want: a state of effortless flow.

Self-Talk

I truly believe that self-talk is one of the most powerful but also underutilised resources you have to create a peak-performance mindset. When you make a mistake, do you default to beating yourself up with internal verbal abuse? Or can you be kind, pick yourself up and encourage yourself to get back to the task at hand? The way you speak to yourself matters, because you can build yourself up or tear yourself down. Your self-talk reflects whether you will be your own best friend or worst enemy.

> "Death and life are in the power of the tongue."
>
> – Proverbs 18:21

Powerful positive self-talk is a tool that's long been used by overachievers. Positive self-talk has the potential to reprogramme and replace limiting beliefs. Choosing to love and be kind to yourself sets you up for greater success, just as believing that you can achieve your goals helps you to do so. Go back to the tabletop method in Chapter 25, and use affirmations to strengthen your new beliefs about yourself.[20]

> "I am: two of the most powerful words; for what you put after them shapes your reality."
>
> – Bevan Lee

I start with my affirmations every morning before I get out of bed. I have a book full of them; as I think of new ones, I add them to the list. These are some of my favourites:

I am a powerful creator. I am worthy, loved and whole. I am more than enough as I am. I am supported and guided. I am unstoppable in achieving my goals. I am abundantly blessed and so grateful for the life I live.

As I read them out loud, I always feel a shift in my state. Any time during the day that I feel like I'm being thrown off track, I come back to them.

My affirmations are a strong reminder to me of what is important. I am declaring powerful statements over my life, and my subconscious is taking them in. After my affirmation routine, I always feel alive, happy, grateful and filled with purpose.

Try it; you won't be sorry.

Visualisation

Where affirmations are a verbal cue, visualisation is a visual cue to your own subconscious.

When you visualise, you allow your mind to see the outcomes that you desire. The brain doesn't know the difference between something real and something imagined—so when you visualise something, you are indicating to your mind that it already exists. This summons all kinds of subconscious processes to your aid.

So when you are setting out to accomplish even a small goal, close your eyes and practise the art of experiencing it in your mind. See how effortlessly you complete the task, and sense how much gratitude you feel during and after the process.

Reflection

Everyone needs time to look back and reflect on their lives—it's when we don't do this that life passes us by in a blur.

Introspection feeds awareness. Often, we focus so much on the doing that we forget we are human beings. Reflection is all about becoming more aware, and the greatest portion of growth comes out of awareness. The more aware you become, the more you can grow in every area of your life.

> "Time spent in self-reflection is never wasted – it is an intimate date with yourself."
>
> – Dr Paul T P Wong

When you are taking the time to reflect, create a space that is sacred to you. This is time for you to carve out a moment of peace and tranquillity, where you can just come back to yourself.

Make sure you're in a peaceful setting where you won't be distracted by the outside world—your phone, family, TV and the like.

This is a time to just sit with your own thoughts. Be present in the moment, and focus on your breath.

We spend so much time thinking of the past or the future that it will be natural for your thoughts to wander. Don't worry too much about that. Observe where they go and, as you do, just bring yourself back to your breath, to the stillness that surrounds you.

For some people, the vital practice of reflection comes in the form of yoga or meditation. Find what works for you and what you feel comfortable with. You can use a guided meditation online, or you can do a seated or even walking meditation. Writing, art, swimming in the ocean—anything that brings you back into the present moment can be a place for reflection.

In the early days of my recovery, I found that journalling really helped me. This was a process where, instead of internalising my feelings, I could get them out onto a page. For many years, I had taught myself to bury the feelings or thoughts I didn't like, so this felt incredibly liberating. Writing became a therapeutic outlet for me. In the process, I released many of the challenges I thought I had—by getting them out of my head and onto the page in front of me, they seemed to dissolve.

Mental Exercise

Your mind works just like a muscle. The more you stimulate your neurons, the more they fire together and the stronger they become.

The same way you need to move your body every day, commit to stretching your mind. You may enjoy reading, listening to an audiobook, doing an online course, attending a face-to-face workshop, even studying a certificate course or degree.

Build up simple mental habits like reading a book or listening to an audiobook for 30 minutes before bed. It's fine to take a break and watch some TV—but instead of bingeing six episodes of a Netflix series, check out a YouTube interview with someone you admire, or a clip on a topic that interests you. Instead of playing the same music on repeat while driving, subscribe to podcasts. (You'll find a list of my favourites in the "Further Resources" section at the back of this book.) When you use this time to feed your mind and build up mental muscle, traffic suddenly becomes a pleasure.

In my cycle of addiction, especially after each relapse, it was books that pulled me through. I read Dr John Demartini's *The Gratitude Effect* and Wayne Dyer's *The Power of Intention*, and I'd feel my energy shift from hopelessness to a renewed sense of strength and excitement.

Remember, you don't have to do it all overnight. Don't bite off more than you can chew. Buy your first book, and be disciplined about reading for 15 minutes a day. As you begin to implement some of the wise tips you pick up, you'll

> "Reading is to the mind what exercise is to the body."
> – Joseph Addison

be inspired to deepen your commitment. Soon it will become a habit—and then you will see the fruits of your efforts.

Chapter 46
Peak Performance Habits for Your Soul

So, your body's firing on all cylinders, your mindset's razor-sharp and focused on the task ahead—now let's set up some fail-safe habits to make sure your heart and soul are full, aligned and in support of your cause.

When it comes to cultivating peak performance habits that feed your soul, I'm talking about anything that awakens love, connection, purpose and a sense of belonging. Tapping into your soul is about coming back home, back to self. It's the process of getting in touch with the source that lies within you—a source of immense internal power and stability.

Connection

You weren't created to journey through this life alone. None of us was. On a soul level, we're all connected as a group consciousness that shares this beautiful human experience. Many have walked this path, and there are many you can learn from. Love and connection are real human needs.

As we saw in Chapter 35, the people closest to you have a major impact on your wellbeing. Do you hold each other back from your goals, or do you push one another forward towards them? You need to be intentional about the people you want to be close to, because fostering and growing healthy connections and creating a support structure is vital, especially when times are tough.

> "You are the average of the five people you spend the most time with."
> – Jim Rohn

Think of the difference between a friend who just wants to pull you out to party and one who will bring over a meal when you have a huge deadline looming.

Who do you want to be surrounded by? Who can you learn from who's already walked the path you are on? What mentors can you seek out in your industry?

Your VIP support structure is so important. In my case, I have the most incredible friends with whom I can be honest, open and vulnerable. They remind me who I am and point me towards my purpose, so there's no space for guilt or shame to grow in my life.

Coming out of rehab, I was blessed to have incredible mentors in the property space who I could learn from. Any time I was unsure of what to do, I'd have coffee with one of them. I found I had years of wisdom and experience at my fingertips, and I know there were many mistakes I avoided because I had such incredible sounding boards. I always made sure I added even more value back into their lives, and was always eager to help wherever I could.

Whatever you do, don't push people away because of some idea that you need to knuckle down and walk this path alone. Don't isolate yourself. It's healthy to have people to share your journey with, people you can confide in, who will encourage you and nudge you forward. Invest in your connections and tap into an immense source of support.

Spend Time Alone

Just as growing deeper connections with others is important, so is having time for yourself—time to reflect, to contemplate your journey and to come back to your inner being. Remember that within your veins flows the creative force of the universe. You already have everything you will ever need to succeed and be happy. Often we are so consumed by the outside world, so busy, that we forget to create the time and space to come back home to ourselves. To just be still and listen.

Maybe you struggle to be alone. When I was stuck in my mess, I couldn't be alone—the sheer thought of it awakened severe anxiety and fear. When we do the work of ownership and begin to adopt healthy emotions, we change our state. As you grow in various areas of your life, you will find that time alone becomes incredibly precious—and you actually begin to enjoy it.

Treat yourself like you would your best friend—because that is what you should be. Run yourself a bubble bath, book yourself a massage, take yourself for dinner or go see a movie. Just you.

Making space for voluntary periods of solitude can actually improve your relationships with others; it also fosters higher levels of empathy, creativity and productivity. It's incredibly powerful to be able to sit by yourself with nothing but your own thoughts.

An Attitude of Gratitude

I've always kept a gratitude journal. I started in the middle of my messy twenties. I'm still blown away when I page through my old journals and discover that many of the things I was grateful for soon materialised in my life.

Gratitude raises your happiness, and shifts your focus to areas of your life where you can experience deep appreciation and love. When someone is thinking of something they are grateful for, their energetic field has been measured to extend more than three metres beyond their body.[21]

Gratitude should be practised daily, because the more you are grateful for what you have, the more you are given to be grateful for. Gratitude for what you already have is also a powerful tool for grounding yourself in the present moment.

> "Some people grumble that roses have thorns; I am grateful that thorns have roses."
>
> – Jean-Baptiste Alphonse Karr

Do Things You Love

The more you come into alignment with your authentic self, the more powerful you feel and the more connected you are to yourself, which shines through as confidence. This links back to having discipline: doing the things that need to be done in order to get to where you want to be.

Let go of people-pleasing and come into alignment with what you truly desire. Start saying no to the things that no longer reflect your purpose or keep you on the right path. If knocking back six tequilas on a weeknight doesn't gel with you anymore because you respect your body and want to be at peak performance the next day, just say no. It doesn't matter what people think. They're not running your race for you. It's your journey and your choice to do things that feed your soul.

Sam Cowen, my performance coach, asks all her clients one question: "What makes you happy?" Then she sets up systems so they can do more of what they love.

It sounds simple, but for many people it takes a lot of effort to figure out what actually makes them happy. Do you know what makes you happy? Is it spending time with family, working in the garden, reading in the sun, baking with your children? How can you set up your life so you can do more of that?

TAKE ACTION!

To make doing things you love a habit, you need to write down the things you love to do. Next, you need to create the time to do them more often.

Voilà!

There is a love triangle here—and I'm not talking about a threesome! You have love for yourself, love for others and love for what you do. In the centre is where you will find true contentment.

Feeding your soul is choosing to do more of the things you love, more often.

Give Back

Whenever I speak to anyone who is stuck in their head, I give them a simple solution—go and help someone else. On your journey of becoming the person you are destined to be, it's important that you contribute to the world around you—which is another human need.

There's a beautiful part of your soul that awakens when you serve others, especially when all you can get in return is the joy of that moment. I truly believe this is our greatest purpose and the primary reason we are placed in this world— to help others, to rise by lifting others with us. It feels so good to be of service. Apart from making the world a better place, it makes you a better person too.

There are so many ways you can roll up your sleeves and give of your time to those less fortunate than you. You can volunteer at an animal shelter, soup kitchen or beach clean-up, or help out at a children's or old-age home. Think of a cause that is close to your heart. Maybe you had a loved one die of cancer, and you'd like to get involved in that area. Whatever it is, reach out—and I guarantee you will find a way to contribute.

Helping others awakens your sense of purpose, gives you perspective, boosts your self-esteem and makes you feel plugged in to humanity. When you serve others, your soul sings—and love overflows.

Chapter 47
Rejection or Redirection

For as long as you are alive, you will face pain, obstacles and challenges—they are vital for your growth. You don't wake up at a certain age to find that everything is perfect.

This means that as you go into the world excited to birth your plans and goals, you may come across people who turn you down and say no. I'd like you to banish the word "rejection" from your vocabulary, and to understand that every "no"—every time you are turned away—is merely a redirection. It's preventing you from playing small, and shifting your focus to where it needs to be. It's guiding you to the right investors, the right clients, the right locations, the perfect moment of alignment where magic is going to happen.

When a door closes, you may want to stand in front of it, knocking until your knuckles bleed. Stop. Walk down the corridor and go through the door that's wide open, waiting for you.

It's not your setbacks that define you, it's how you handle them. It's your ability to bounce back. Resilience is the name of the game.

If you are launching a product, service or idea into the world, you're going to need a thick skin and the ability to keep moving forward, no matter how many times you think you're faltering.

Remember Jack Ma's story in Chapter 8? How many times can one human endure rejection? But he wasn't being rejected, was he? He was being redirected to the moment in his life where Alibaba would catapult him to becoming the richest man in China and one of the richest men in the world.

Similarly, Jeff Bezos, Elon Musk, Oprah Winfrey, JK Rowling, Warren Buffett and the Beatles were all rejected multiple times before they became world-changing success stories.[22]

Come up with a ritual for every time you get a "no". Create a catch-phrase or mantra to remind yourself that it's okay, that you can be thankful that you are being redirected to an even better path. Play, have fun and don't for a second allow someone else's opinion or judgment to stop you in your tracks.

Keep moving forward, stay resolute on your vision, and know that your time is coming. Your goal is just around the corner!

SUMMARY OF ACTION

In this section, we have examined a number of important ideas that will bring your vision to life and set you up for a life of excellence.

- Action is what makes your vision a reality.
- This is where the rubber meets the road—and it's where most people give up.
- Only one in 10 people will take action towards their dream life.
- Fear, procrastination, people and perfectionism are your biggest barriers to taking action.
- Discipline is the secret sauce and the only way to see real progress.
- Personal integrity, how you show up for yourself, matters even in the little things.
- You have to start small and create sustainable habits that become automatic.
- There is tremendous power when you stack small decisions and actions together.
- You need to take action and strike when your idea is hot.
- You have to choose between comfort or calling—you cannot have both.
- Your brain seeks to move away from pain towards pleasure, which often affects your ability to take action.
- To consistently take action, you need to adopt peak performance habits for your body, mind and soul.
- There is no such thing as a rejection, only a redirection to something even greater.

Conclusion
Making a Commitment to Yourself

We'vecome to the end of our journey. Now it's time to take these tools and set them in motion. If you feel moved by what you've read, and if you are ready to step into your future, then maybe right now is the moment you need to make a commitment.

Commit that you will take radical *ownership* of your past and for your present—that you will let go of patterns, thoughts, feelings and behaviours that don't serve you.

Commit to crafting a *vision* for your life that will not only set you up for success and happiness, but will leave a legacy for generations to come—a *vision* so grand that your eight-year-old and 80-year-old self would be proud.

Commit that you will take *action* to do whatever it takes to achieve that vision. You will become a peak performer with habits that set you up for success, excellence and victory as you smash your goals out of the park.

Lastly, commit to being kind to yourself on your journey, and to being kinder to others.

I am glad you came on this journey with me. You are deserving and worthy of stepping into the highest version of yourself. When you commit to this proccss, you will watch in awc as your lifc transforms around you. You don't ever need to feel stuck again. You can welcome pain, obstacles and challenges into your life because you know they are there for you to stretch and grow. As you master these lessons and contribute positively to the world around you, you will be able to show others how to do it in their own lives—the student will become the teacher.

No matter where you find yourself today, know that you are destined for greatness.

Now go out there and make yourself proud. You've got everything it takes. It's your time to shine.

Bibliography

Antanaityte, Neringa. "Mind Matters: How to Effortlessly Have More Positive Thoughts". tlexinstitute.com/how-to-effortlessly-have-more-positive-thoughts (Accessed 6 September 2021).

Bilyeu, Tom and Lisa. Impact Theory. impacttheory.com.

Brown, Brené. The Gifts of Imperfection: Let go of who you think you're supposed to be and embrace who you are. London: Vermillion (2020).

Buggy, Patrick. "The Power of Perception: Change Your Narrative, Change Your Life". mindfulambition.net/wp-content/uploads/wp-post-to-pdf-enhanced-cache/1/power-of-perception.pdf (Accessed 6 September 2021).

Byrne, Rhonda. The Secret. Oregon: Atria Books/Beyond Words (2006).

Clear, James. "Core values list". jamesclear.com/core-values (Accessed 6 September 2021).

Clive, Bernard Kelvin. Your Dreams Will Not Die. lulu.com (2006) Demartini, John. The Gratitude Effect. Berkeley: Stone Bridge Press (2008) Dispenza, Joe. You Are the Placebo: Making Your Mind Matter. Carlsbad: Hay House (2014).

Dyer, Wayne. The Power of Intention: Learning to Co-create Your World Your Way. Carlsbad: Hay House (2005).

Ferriss, Tim. Tools of Titans: The Tactics, Routines, and Habits of Billionaires, Icons, and World-Class Performers. Boston: Mariner Books (2016).

Ferriss, Tim. Tribe of Mentors: Short Life Advice from the Best in the World. Boston: Mariner Books (2017).

Gottschall, Jonathan. The Storytelling Animal: How Stories Make Us Human. Boston: Mariner Books (2013).

Greene, Robert. The Laws of Human Nature. London: Profile Books (2018)

Hicks, Esther & Jerry. Ask and It Is Given: Learning to Manifest Your Desires. Carlsbad: Hay House (2004).

Huber, Liz. "20 Limiting Beliefs that Mess with Your Dreams". medium.com/@refinedliz/20-limiting-beliefs-that-mess-with-your-dreams-b4cfeb2f66ca (Accessed 6 September 2021).

Keithly, Zanna, "How to Use Affirmations (So They Actually Work)". zannakeithley.com/2020/10/22/how-to-use-affirmations (Accessed 6 September 2021).

Ledwell, Natalie. "30 Good Habits for Peak Daily Performance". mindmovies.com/blogroll/30-good-habits-for-daily-peak-performance (Accessed 6 September 2021).

Maraboli, Steve. Unapologetically You: Reflections on Life and Human Experience. New York: A Better Today (2013).

Pattakos, Alex. Prisoners of Our Thoughts: Viktor Frankl's Principles for Discovering Meaning in Life and Work. Oakland: Berrett-Koehler Publishers (2010).

Proctor, Bob. "How your mind works". proctorgallagherinstitute.com/25593/how-your-mind-works (Accessed 6 September 2021).

Proctor, Bob. "How to create a compelling life script". proctorgallagherinstitute.com/17131/how-to-create-a-compelling-life-script (Accessed 6 September 2021).

Robbins, Anthony. Awaken the Giant Within: How to Take Immediate Control of Your Mental, Emotional, Physical and Financial Destiny! New York: Simon & Schuster (1993).

Robbins, Mel. The 5 Second Rule: Transform Your Life, Work, and Confidence with Everyday Courage. Brentwood: Permuted Press (2017).

Rohn, Jim. "Take Action (Motivational Speech That May Change Your Life)", youtube.com/watch?v=3cOaE84NJT8 (Accessed 6 September 2021).

Siddiq, Adam. "145 inspiring quotes for peak performance in your life". adamsiddiq.com/2015/10/145-peak-performance-quotes (Accessed 6 September 2021).

Sharma, Robin. The 5am Club: Own Your Morning, Elevate Your Life. New York: HarperCollins (2018).

Trautwein, Kayla. "The Most Common Limiting Beliefs and How You Can Overcome Them". Medium.com/@kaylatrautwein/the-most-common-limiting-beliefs-and-how-you-can-overcome-them-c294b1871009 (Accessed 6 September 2021).

Tracy, Brian. No Excuses!: The Power of Self-Discipline. New York: Vanguard Press (2011).

Zipkin, Nina. "Stories of Rejection From 8 of the World's Most Successful Entrepreneurs and Leaders". Entrepreneur.com/article/311319 (Accessed 6 September 2021).

Further Resources

For more inspiration, have a look at the work of the following trailblazers:

Bob Proctor – proctorgallagherinstitute.com

Brené Brown – brenebrown.com.

Eckhart Tolle – eckharttolle.com

Grant Cardone – grantcardone.com

Jim Rohn – jimrohn.com.

Dr Joe Dispenza – drjoedispenza.com.

The Law of Attraction – thelawofattraction.com

Peggy McColl – go.peggymccoll.com/home-start

PSYCH-K® – psych-k.com.

Tim Ferriss – tim.blog.

Tom and Lisa Bilyeu – impacttheory.com

Tony Robbins – tonyrobbins.com.

My favourite podcasts and shows are:

Lewis Howes, "School of Greatness Podcast" – lewishowes.com/sogpodcast

Reid Hoffman, "Masters of Scale" – mastersofscale.com.

Robin Sharma, "The Mastery Sessions" – robinsharma.com/podcast Tom Bilyeu, "Impact Theory" – impacttheory.com/episodes.

Tony Robbins, "The Tony Robbins Podcast" – tonyrobbins.com/podcasts.

For more resources mentioned in this book, go to: *devonbrough.com/get-ova-it*

End Notes

[1] tlexinstitute.com/how-to-effortlessly-have-more-positive-thoughts.

[2] This is a concept Dr Joe Dispenza has repeated many times on different platforms. This particular quote comes from his fan page on Facebook: facebook.com/DrJoeDispenzaOfficialNewsFanPage/posts/489097081115691./ (Accessed 6 September 2021).

[3] Based on content from Patrick Buggy's article "The Power of Perception: Change Your Narrative, Change Your Life": mindfulambition.net/wp-content/uploads/wp-post-to-pdf-enhanced-cache/1/power-of-perception.pdf.

[4] Based on Kirk Franklin's message on Twitter: twitter.com/kirkfranklin/status/291196483334729729.

[5] From Patrick Buggy, "The Power of Perception: Change Your Narrative, Change Your Life": mindfulambition.net/wp-content/uploads/wp-post-to-pdf-enhanced-cache/1/power-of-perception.pdf.

[6] The first plane struck the North Tower between floors 93 and 99 at 8.46am, and no-one on the higher floors survived. Those who died included all 658 employees of the financial-services firm Cantor Fitzgerald who had arrived for work that day—but CEO Howard Lutnick was not among them. He was running late, having had to take his son to his first day of kindergarten: wikipedia.org/wiki/Cantor_Fitzgerald

[7] This list is adapted from jamesclear.com.

[8] Taken from a list by Liz Huber in her article "20 Limiting Beliefs that Mess with Your Dreams": medium.com/@refinedliz/20-limiting-beliefs-that-mess-with-your-dreams-b4cfeb2f66ca

[9] Find out more at psych-k.com.

[10] Adapted from "The Most Common Limiting Beliefs and How You Can Overcome them" by Kayla Trautwein: medium.com/@kaylatrautwein/the-most-common-limiting-beliefs-and-how-you-can-overcome-them-c294b1871009.

[11] Bob Proctor explains in more detail how this process works and provides powerful illustrations—it's worth looking it up: proctorgallagherinstitute.com/25593/how-your-mind-works.

[12] For more from Peggy McColl, go to her website: go.peggymccoll.com/ home-start. At the time of writing, The Power Life Script Quick Start Guide was available at go.peggymccoll.com/powerlifescript-ebook32645209.

[13] Bob Proctor explains the process at proctorgallagherinstitute.com/ 17131/how-to-create-a-compelling-life-script.

[14] Ibid.

[15] According to a number of websites, the first recorded use of the SMART acronym was by George T Doran in an article titled "There's a S.M.A.R.T. way to write management's goals and objectives", which appeared in Management Review in November 1981.

[16] Jim Rohn speaks about this on YouTube—watch his video "Take Action (Motivational Speech That May Change Your Life)": youtube.com/watch?v=3cOaE84NJT8.

[17] This is a version of "the wheat/rice on the chessboard problem", in which a grain of wheat or rice is placed on the first square of a chessboard and the number is doubled from there: two on the second, four on the third, eight on the fourth, and so on. With 64 squares on the board, the end result is more than 1.4-trillion tons of wheat—more than 2 000 times the annual world production!

[18] For a video of this speech, look up "Jim Rohn Law of Diminishing Intent" on YouTube—there are many versions available. I watched "Take Action (Motivational Speech That May Change Your Life)": youtube.com/watch?v=3cOaE84NJT8

[19] Have a look at his website: grantcardone.com.

[20] For a great guide to using affirmations, and affirmations for every occasion, go to zannakeithley.com.

[21] Dr Joe Dispenza discusses the idea of gratitude and abundance on YouTube—check out the video "Gratitude and How It Creates Abundance": youtube.com/watch?v=HWLuNvcoLHo

[22] To read more on each of their stories, go to Nina Zipkin's article "Stories of Rejection from 8 of the World's Most Successful Entrepreneurs and Leaders" on entrepreneur.com

Ingram Content Group UK Ltd.
Milton Keynes UK
UKHW020638220623
423865UK00007B/376